THE BEDSIDE ARK

David
Muirhead

Illustrations by
Patricia de Villiers

FOR JEMIMA ROSE

Published by Struik Nature
(an imprint of Penguin Random House South Africa (Pty) Ltd)
Reg. No. 1953/000441/07
The Estuaries No. 4, Oxbow Crescent, Century Avenue, Century City, 7441
PO Box 1144, Cape Town, 8000 South Africa

Visit www.randomstruik.co.za and join the Struik Nature Club
for updates, news, events and special offers.

1 3 5 7 9 10 8 6 4 2

Publisher: Pippa Parker
Managing editor: Helen de Villiers
Editor: Emily Donaldson
Concept and cover design: Janice Evans
Illustrator: Patricia de Villiers
Typesetter: Deirdré Geldenhuys
Decorative rules designed by Freepik.com

Reproduction by Hirt & Carter Cape (Pty) Ltd
Printed and bound by DJE Flexible Print Solutions (Pty) Ltd

Print: 978 1 77584 461 7
ePub: 978 1 77584 462 4
ePDF: 978 1 77584 463 1

CONTENTS

PREFACE

I wrote this book for people interested in the natural world who are looking for something a little different from the standard collection of animal CVs. It is not a guide or a reference book in the traditional sense, but I hope you'll discover things about the creatures in these pages you didn't know before. I also hope you'll come to see them a little differently, perhaps as fellow travellers on life's rocky road rather than simply as wayside zoological curiosities.

I've called it *The Bedside Ark*, because I think it's the kind of book people can enjoy at bedtime, a sanctuary of sorts from the deluge of horrors on the evening news. We live in ominous times and though I sincerely doubt a big booming voice from the clouds will personally command me to get my carpentry kit out, there's no harm in drawing up a preliminary passenger list, just in case. This is mine.

It's a motley collection to be sure, not the sort of methodical list Noah laboriously ticked off on his clipboard. Thinking of that, I've always wondered which expletives the zebras used when they heard that embarkation on the original Ark was going to be in strict alphabetical order. Given the queue ahead of them at the time their remarks were probably unrepeatable. They didn't have to wait as long to climb aboard these pages.

I've dedicated the book to my granddaughter, Jemima Rose, who is four months old at the time of writing. Goodness knows what the world will be like when she reaches my age. What I do know is that all the creatures in this book – and all those that aren't – against the odds will have used all the wiles and talents Nature gave them to try to make sure their descendants get to that faraway day. I fervently hope they succeed.

There is an erudite and largely unsung army of men and women, too numerous to acknowledge here, who have dedicated their lives to getting to know and understand the diminishing wild world and, with a mounting sense of urgency, to convey that understanding to the rest of us. Virtually all the facts and figures in this book I owe to them. What has become clear to me during my research is that there are many things about wild creatures that are probably unknowable in the end, and for the sake of sanity, theirs and ours, that's probably how it should be. They are the tenacious keepers of mysteries and secrets in a world that is rapidly being laid bare and stripped of wonder.

I'd like to thank Pippa Parker and her colleagues at Penguin Random House for having faith in this book and for doing such a great job of putting it together. I'd also like to thank my wife Marie for helping with the research, not least by struggling back and forth to the library with heavy tomes. If you've ever accidentally dropped a copy of David Attenborough's *The Trials of Life* on your foot you'll know what a dangerous and arduous task that can be. Last but not least I'd like to thank you for picking up this book. I hope you enjoy it.

DAVID MUIRHEAD

AARDVARK

One dubious advantage of being an aardvark is that you're always at the top of any alphabetical list, which is strangely appropriate for an animal that is truly one of a kind, the sole member of the obscure mammalian order Tubulidentata. I can also tell you that aardvarks are a fossil species, though that's not something they are personally aware of or would probably give a box of ants about. When you can dig a hole 1.5 metres deep in about 60 seconds you don't need to worry about being called a mammalian antique.

Magicians of the Hausa people in Nigeria hold the aardvark's ability to vanish into the ground in such high esteem that they make and sell charms out of bits of it – ground-up skin, heart and nails. The aardvark would probably prefer to be less admired. The charm is worn around the neck and gives the wearer the ability to walk through walls. Gullible burglars are presumably the main customers.

The animal's physical appearance is bizarre enough to tax even the finest descriptive talents. It looks as though it's made of leftovers. In English it's known as an ant bear, even though there's nothing remotely bearish about it; while in Afrikaans the name aardvark means 'earth pig', and this animal does indeed have some piggy features, including a piggy snout and relatively hairless pale skin, which is usually stained reddish-pink with dust.

But there the resemblance ends. It has a longish, hairless, tapering tail, thick at the base, a bit like that of a giant rat. While we're about it we could probably throw in a bit of sloth (heavy-duty claws), jackrabbit (huge, all-the-better-to-hear-you-with ears) and a smidgen of scaled-up shrew (long, pointy snout). It is out and about only after dark and, as there are no mirrors underground, is probably not too fussed about the fact that it's no raving beauty.

The aardvark's least endearing feature is its 30-centimetre, fully retractable sticky tongue – the last thing ants and termites want to see snaking around the corner of one of their tunnels. Using its spade-like claws, it can crack open a rock-hard termite mound with consummate ease to lap up breakfast, lunch and dinner. Claims have been made that an aardvark can consume 50,000 termites in a single night, though precisely how such an exact and methodical count was ever achieved is a moot point.

The furious stinging and biting counterattacks mounted by ants and termites are rendered irrelevant by the aardvark's thick skin.

The nutritious, if monotonous, diet is only varied by the occasional consumption of a mysterious type of cucumber, *Cucumis humifructus*, which fruits underground and is largely dependent on aardvarks to spread its seeds via their droppings. It chomps the fruit with a set of peg-like rootless teeth at the back of its elongated jaw. The complicated dentition of the aardvark could easily be the subject of a dentistry thesis, which, alas, has no place in a bedside book.

And nor, possibly, does sex, but since you're curious, suffice it to say that aardvarks are solitary beasts and pair only during the breeding season. The female gives birth to a single cub after a gestation period of seven months. The cub is weaned by 16 weeks and then it's straight onto the termites and cucumbers. It usually stays with the mother, sharing her burrow until the next mating season, but is fully capable of digging its own burrow after a mere six months.

Though you might live your whole life in Africa without ever laying eyes on one, aardvarks are relatively ubiquitous south of the Sahara, making a nocturnal living wherever there are ants and termites and earth to burrow into. They are the realtors of the bushveld, passing on second-hand but highly desirable subterranean homes to a variety of other animals, including wild dogs and warthogs. The main burrow can be extensive, relatively capacious and have several entrances. Like any sensible homeowner, the aardvark makes continual modifications and improvements.

Apart from Hausa magicians and other African peoples who hunt aardvarks for the pot, their main worries are lions, leopards and wild dogs. Their keen senses of smell and hearing give them warning of approaching danger, but when they are surprised out in the open, and don't have time to dig like crazy, they run a confusing zigzag course, presumably hoping that their pursuer will get dizzy and give up. If all else fails they fight back with their claws, but given the superior arsenal and lethal efficiency of their principal predators, that's usually not enough.

HONEYBEE

Bees are born from the tears of the sun, or so the Ancient Egyptians believed. This mystical insight probably has something to do with the fact that honey, the product of bees' incessant labour, is as close to liquid sunlight as it's possible to get. Bees need to visit upwards of 50,000 flowers to produce enough honey to spread on your morning toast, something to bear in mind when you're standing in the aisle of a supermarket scratching your backside and mumbling about the price.

Maybe you can do without honey, but if there weren't bees, there wouldn't be any marmalade or jam either. In fact, there wouldn't be a whole lot of other things. The best estimate is that bees pollinate about a third of all food crops consumed by human beings. Put another way, if bees vanished, so would a lot of the food you eat. And it's worth bearing in mind that domestic animals also depend to a large extent on food crops, so you could expect a big problem with your bacon and eggs as well.

Honeybees are members of the order Hymenoptera, which includes bumblebees, wasps, sawflies and ants. South Africa is home to two subspecies of honeybee, the African bee *(Apis mellifera scutellata)* and the Cape bee *(Apis mellifera capensis)*, with the latter generally confined to the fynbos of the western and southern Cape and the former covering the rest of the country. In between is a hybridization zone where strange things can happen, but more of that later.

The social life of bees has often been compared with that of human societies, in a rather garbled and half-baked attempt to make sense of how and why we organize ourselves into hierarchies, i.e. why most of us have to work our arses off from dawn to dusk while the boss gets to drive a Ferrari and play golf. For the bees themselves, such social inequalities are not a conundrum. The undisputed head of a bee colony is the queen, who secures her privileged position by secreting a special pheromone that inhibits the sexual development of workers, while simultaneously inducing in them a sense of social wellbeing.

There are three types of bee in a hive: the queen, the worker bees, which are all female, and the drones, which are all male. Drones are born from unfertilized eggs and have no stinger, pollen basket or wax glands. They tend to eat more than the workers and hence are bigger. Other than that, virtually their only purpose is to mate with queen bees. Feminist readers can take comfort from the fact that drones are usually booted out of the hive in autumn or when food runs low.

Workers – surprise, surprise – do all the work around the hive, gather food, tend the larvae and defend the colony when it's threatened. Like the queen, they can also lay unfertilized eggs, which hatch as drones. But only the queen can produce future queens, which are differentiated early on by diet. All female larvae are initially fed royal jelly, a nutrient-rich substance. Those destined to become workers – the great majority – are soon switched to a more modest diet of pollen and honey. Only the future queens are fed royal jelly throughout the larval stage.

When they're ready, the virgin queens leave the hive, heading for the bee equivalent of the red-light district, where drones hang out, and all the while they emit that magic pheromone. Mating takes place in flight, between 3 and 12 metres above ground. It is literally an explosive affair, occasionally audible to the human ear, and fatal for the drones. The queen mates with 7–10 individual drones, each allotted about two or three seconds. The result of this brief aerial orgy is that the queen is able to store enough sperm within her oviducts to last her for the rest of her life, during which she will selectively lay thousands of eggs and reign supreme over a new colony.

Cape bees can be distinguished from African bees by their darker abdomen and passing resemblance to an African bee queen. They also have an unusual characteristic in that workers are capable of laying both male and female eggs, so that if the queen dies, a successor can be raised to take her place. The downside of these characteristics is that if a Cape bee worker arrives in an African bee colony she is not attacked, and, uninhibited by the hive queen's pheromones, soon begins producing exact replicas of herself. The resultant social disorder ultimately leads to the collapse of the colony.

Worldwide, bees have bigger problems. In recent years a variety of factors, natural and artificial, have combined to put bees in harm's way. New parasite and virus strains are attacking hives, while the increased use of pesticides is having a serious impact on bees' health and immune systems. Compounding these problems, urban sprawl in many parts of the world has led to a marked decrease in available foraging sites, and noise and electromagnetic pollution cause considerable stress to bees, making them more susceptible to infection.

One pertinent piece of folklore tells us that if a bee flies into your house, it means that someone is coming to visit. If you kill the bee, the visitor will bring you bad news. There is no need here to belabour the ominous moral of that short story.

OCTOPUS

According to a Hawaiian creation myth, the present universe was cobbled together from the wreck of a previous cosmos. The sole survivor of that alien otherworld is the octopus. It's an easy myth to believe, especially if you're diving on the shattered remains of a sunken ship and come eyeball to eyeball with one of these creatures. Such encounters are the stuff of most folks' nightmares but are probably just as alarming for the octopus.

Octopuses (as opposed to the plural octopi, which is etymologically controversial) are solitary and retiring cephalopod molluscs that have famously devised a number of neat tricks to stay out of harm's way. The first of these is not to be seen in the first place. Unlike other cephalopods, octopuses have no internal or external hard parts, other than their parrot-like beaks, and are thus able to ooze into unbelievably tight spaces from which they can inconspicuously watch the predatory world go by.

All octopuses have specialized skin cells that are able to draw on demand from a palette of pigments – yellow, red, orange, brown or black – to colour their skin to match their surroundings. Some species also have the muscular ability to change the texture of their skin and so blend in completely with lumpy rocks, knobbly seaweeds or the detritus on the sea floor. By and large, octopuses that are active in daylight hours and live in complex environments such as coral reefs have evolved these abilities to a greater degree than their sand-dwelling, nocturnal cousins. A few have attained a peak of contortionism that enables them to rearrange their bodies to resemble something nastier than they are, such as a lion fish or a sea snake.

When it is discovered and targeted by a predator, typically a moray eel, a shark or an agent of the Yamomoto Calamari Canning

Company, the octopus rummages around in its remaining bag of tricks. First off, it releases a cloud of ink, which isn't really ink at all, being mainly composed of melanin – the same stuff that gives us our hair and skin colour and protects the skin from sun damage – so you could say it's more akin to suntan lotion. It also contains a substance that inhibits the enemy's sense of smell. In some instances the ink cloud is thought to act as a pseudomorph, a bit like a matador's cloak, providing an alternative target for the puzzled predator. Hidden behind all this commotion, the octopus takes off like a rocket by pumping a jet of water through its mantle.

In extremis, and when all else fails, some species have a final trick up one of their eight sleeves. Like some lizards, they can deftly detach an arm, a relatively innocuous sacrifice, given that the arm soon grows back, no harm done.

Life for the octopus is not just about avoiding being something else's lunch. Octopuses are highly effective predators themselves. There are about 300 species of octopus and all of them, to a lesser rather than a greater degree, are venomous. The one you most want to avoid upsetting, especially if you hail from Down Under, is the blue-ringed octopus, the only one known to be lethal to humans. A tiny 25-gram blue ring has enough tetrodotoxin to paralyse the entire Australian cricket team, so if you're a mollusc or a small fish your chances of surviving the innings are not very promising.

Octopus venom is delivered via their saliva and is employed to subdue prey so that it can be conveniently chopped up into manageable portions by the beak. The octopus's staple diet consists of crabs, crayfish and molluscs, though larger specimens extend their menu to include fish, even small sharks, and, if the opportunity arises, an occasional inattentive seabird.

Despite the best efforts of Hollywood, there is no plausible evidence that octopuses drag down ships to snack on the hapless crew. It would be no mean feat, given that the average common octopus (rather unfairly described as *Octopus vulgaris*) weighs in at a modest 3–10 kilograms and

spans 30–91 centimetres with its arms out. The exception is the giant Pacific octopus, which holds the record with an arm span of 9 metres and an impressive weight of 272 kilograms. By contrast, the largest squid so far recorded had a span of 14 metres and weighed more than you want to imagine.

Octopuses are more into brain than brawn. There is little doubt that they are intelligent. Why this should be so is something of a puzzle, given that their cephalopod relatives have the intellectual capacity of a jam sandwich. We humans are fond of bragging about how our opposable thumbs have helped make us marginally brighter than a chimpanzee. That may be so, but it is interesting to note that an octopus can grasp and manipulate an object with each individual sucker – and it has hundreds of them. And while we are social creatures and have the benefit of learning from each other, the octopus is solitary and learns entirely alone.

There are well-documented cases of octopuses using and playing with objects and even solving relatively complex problems, and then remembering how they did it. One enterprising individual climbed out of his aquarium tank during the night to eat the fish in an adjacent tank and then clambered home before dawn. It was some time before puzzled aquarium staff worked out what was going on, and then only because they caught him in the act.

Sex for the octopus is a terminal affair. The male dies within a few weeks of mating, and the female doesn't eat while she is looking after her eggs and then dies of starvation soon after the eggs hatch. On average, octopuses live only for about two years. Perhaps in some strange way having a brief life is the enigmatic creature's way of acknowledging the limited capacity of the earth to sustain life. Maybe the Hawaiians are right, and the octopus really does know what happened to the last world.

DASSIE

If you happen to be introduced to a dassie at a cocktail party, within minutes you'll almost certainly be told that it's closely related to the elephant. You'll hear that the family connection goes back millions of years. It's a humbling bit of information, especially when all you can come up with in the way of distinguished relatives is your Great-uncle Bob who did quite well in the furniture trade back in the 1960s.

The dassie, or rock hyrax as it might prefer to be formally known, doesn't look like an elephant, walk like an elephant or trumpet like an elephant, and of course it isn't an elephant, but it can indeed claim to be a distant relation. When you're a small animal, and most people simply assume that you're a kind of fat rat, that's important.

If you're inclined to take such ancestral bragging with a pinch of salt, pause to consider a few common features. The tusks for a start: most mammalian tusks develop from the canine teeth, but in both dassies and elephants they developed from the incisors, albeit rather more modestly in the case of the dassie. And the feet: both have flattened nails on their digits, unlike the curved claws of other mammals, always excepting a curved grooming claw on the inner toe of the rear feet of the dassie. The elephant doesn't need one of those, having a trunk to do the job. There are also marked similarities down in the reproductive and mammary departments, though not things we talk too loudly about in polite company.

Sadly though, family connections are not always helpful. While the elephant gets to lord it over all, pushing over trees and the occasional tourist minibus and frequently getting its picture into the glossy magazines, the dassie is forced by circumstances to make a modest living in the rocks. It doesn't dig burrows, heaven forbid, rather making intelligent use of the crevices nature haphazardly creates as

16

she disassembles the landscape. Fortunately, that happens a lot, and so the dassie is able to find a home pretty much anywhere in the country.

Dassies are well adapted to their rocky habitat: the padded soles on their sweaty feet act a bit like suction cups, enabling them to walk all over the place, even up the walls. They choose their homes wisely and usually don't have to wander very far to find something to eat. Their diet consists mostly of grass and shrubs, including some that are toxic to other species. When they perceive a threat, such as a lurking caracal or an eagle circling overhead, they can quickly scoot across the patio into the nearest crevice.

They are never at their best in the morning, mainly because they don't have a fixed body temperature. While this adaptation enables them to tolerate a wide range of climatic conditions, it does mean that they're grouchy first thing, would probably kill for a decent cup of coffee and don't want to talk to anyone until they've warmed up in the sun.

When they do get going they chatter quite happily, having at least 21 different sounds, only a couple of which have been translated. A squeal means 'on your marks', and a bark means 'run like hell'. For all we know, the rest of it might include various insults about stuck-up elephants and moans about the injustice of it all.

A family group consists of a dominant male who holds sway over a harem of as many as 15 females, plus assorted youngsters of both sexes. Other mature males live on the periphery or have to set off to find their own digs. This can be a dangerous journey. There are plenty of shady neighbourhood characters with big teeth and talons loitering about, and the dassie is very vulnerable out in the open.

Not that they're always pushovers. Despite their superficially fluffy, toy-store appearance they can be very aggressive, especially when their honour is at stake. 'Australian Tourist in Hospital After Dassie Bites Off Half Her Face', screamed one recent newspaper headline in the finest tradition of over-the-top reporting. It turns out that the dassie bit her nose when she tried to cuddle up for a selfie, but it does go to show it's not wise to take liberties with one of God's own. Battles for dominance between males can get very intense, so much so that the combatants tend to throw caution to the wind and hence become vulnerable to predators.

While a local population may increase quite rapidly under ideal conditions, dassies do not breed like rabbits, at least not in the colloquial sense of that phrase. Females usually give birth to two or three cubs after a seven-month gestation period. The newborns are very precocious and start eating solids within the first few days, though they are not fully weaned for three or four months. I probably shouldn't tell you this, but eating solids includes snacking on pellets from the parental toilet, as a means to acquire bacteria essential for their digestive systems. It's doubtless a touchy subject and maybe something best kept to ourselves.

HONEY BADGER

O ne good thing about honey badgers is that they're not a whole lot bigger, at least if you believe the stories. The bush would be a worrisome place, even if you were a bull elephant.

Folklore is full of tales about the diminutive honey badger bringing down buffalo and other seemingly impossible adversaries – not as prey, but because the animal in question commits some real or imagined provocation. Badgers purportedly have the unnerving habit of honing in on a larger animal's private parts, inflicting injuries bad enough to cause the target of their wrath to bleed to death. No less a personage than James Stevenson-Hamilton, the first warden of the Kruger National Park, reported being a witness to such attacks on wildebeest and waterbuck. They probably don't make crotch guards in jumbo size but if I were a bull elephant I'd maybe go shopping.

Fortunately, the honey badger is a small mammal, weighing in at an average of only 12 kilograms. Badgers have a relatively long lifespan, about 24 years, and females have a relatively long gestation period, around six months. They usually give birth between October and January, producing two cubs. Juvenile honey badgers look just like mom and dad and so, oddly, do cheetah cubs. As a nod to the badger's ferocious reputation, juvenile cheetahs have evolved a similar coloration and hairy profile, only adopting the real cheetah look once they've learned to run like the clappers. Obviously Mother Nature is convinced that at least some of the stories about the badger are true.

As you'd expect from such a resourceful animal, the honey badger is widely distributed in South Africa, and adapted to most

habitats except mountainous forests and deserts. It is usually solitary and is supposed to be nocturnal, though it doesn't always take much notice of that limitation.

Already a film star, the little beast is now also a YouTube sensation, and with good reason. Various film clips show the diminutive hard case facing down a pride of inquisitive lions, lunching on a big poisonous snake and – to prove it has brains as well as brawn – showing off its Houdini skills by easily escaping from cages and enclosures with a nonchalance that embarrasses its human keepers.

Not for nothing did the South African army name one of its most heavily armoured machines the 'Ratel', the honey badger's name in Afrikaans. Tall tales aside, when it comes to rumbles in the jungle, the badger punches way above its weight and more often than not sees off the opposition. A thick, loose hide enables it to take as much punishment as it dishes out, and it is not above emitting a disgusting anal secretion that even the malodorous hyena finds repugnant.

They may not be cuddly, but, let's face it, badgers are cute, and they have a sweet tooth. Honey is a favourite food, though not a staple of their diet. Their fondness for the sweet stuff brings to mind Winnie-the-Pooh, the much-loved, bumbling and amiable hero of A.A. Milne's children's stories. But an obsession with honey is about the only thing the two have in common. The honey badger also eats bee larvae, grubs, scorpions, spiders, birds, snakes, mice and reptiles, to name but a few items on its omnivorous menu. Given the chance, it would probably eat Pooh's tiny friend Piglet rather than have a philosophical conversation with him, and is anything but bumbling while it goes about its daily chores.

As befits its celebrity status, the honey badger occasionally has its own entourage of star-struck hangers-on, including the pale chanting goshawk and the black-backed jackal. In reality – the same reality that usually applies to the groupies clustered around Hollywood's best and brightest – their presence is not so much a case of adulation as perceived opportunity. The badger may be tough, but it is not that agile. When it digs for small rodents, some invariably manage to dash past, their frantic bid for freedom ending abruptly in the jaws or beaks of a member of the highly attentive and nimble audience.

Perhaps the badger's most celebrated and dubious relationship is with the greater honeyguide, a small, inconspicuous bird that science emphatically labels *Indicator indicator,* just in case you missed it the first time. The honeyguide is good at finding beehives but lacks the muscle and chutzpah to exploit the discovery. Enter the hero. The bird sends a tweet to a honey badger ambling about in the vicinity and once it has its attention leads it unerringly to the hive. Given the badger's messy eating habits it's a win-win situation.

Strange things happen in the African bush, but more often than not the badger follows its own agenda and minds its own business. It is not the demon it's sometimes made out to be, but then again, would you make fun of Bruce Willis in a die-hard mood?

HAMERKOP

When a hamerkop is gazing into the water, it is not only looking for fish. Zulu folklore holds that it is also critically examining its own reflection, all the while muttering 'I would have been a handsome fellow, but I am spoiled by this and that'. Most of us will be familiar with the same preoccupation from our teenage years.

Given its uniform dark brown plumage, few would describe the bird as handsome, let alone pretty (both sexes are alike), but the hamerkop has long had ornithologists puzzled. None of them seems quite sure which family to assign it to, so it usually pitches up in books between herons and storks, though it is very different from both.

The hamerkop is widely distributed throughout sub-Saharan Africa, occurring wherever there are ponds, rivers and marshes, even in otherwise arid areas such as the Karoo. It also appears in suburban gardens from time to time, where, undeterred by frightening garden gnomes, it checks out ornamental fish ponds. It can also be seen foraging in rock pools along the coastline. The bulk of the bird's diet consists of fish, though it also enjoys frogs and crustaceans. Hamerkops forage in shallow water, trampling the bottom with their feet to upset the local inhabitants.

On occasion, when three or more birds are feeding together in a small pond, they engage in a strange little dance, skipping around each other and opening and closing their wings in a scene reminiscent of the three witches prancing around the cauldron in *Macbeth*. The point of this weird ritual is not clearly understood; perhaps small fish in the pond creep out to admire the performance and are promptly snapped up at the end of Act 1 Scene 1.

Hamerkops are justly famous for their prodigious nests, which are unlike those of any other bird. A nest can contain a staggering number of twigs and sticks and other bits and pieces, with one estimate putting the total at about 8,000, not far short of the number of bricks needed to build an average three-bedroomed house. The final, impressive structure, which is usually built in a bush or a tree but sometimes on a rock, can weigh up to 50 kilograms and measure a commodious 160 centimetres across and 150 centimetres high. The birds themselves are only 55 centimetres in length. The floor and sides of the nesting chamber as well as the entrance hole are plastered with mud, and a small saucer-shaped depression is created in the rear to hold the eggs. By way of rainproofing, the roof may be covered with a wide array of human rubbish, including tin cans, plastic bags and cardboard.

The birds seem to be obsessive nest-builders, sometimes unnecessarily building two or more in a year. Why they indulge in this time-consuming hobby is yet another mystery to add to the hamerkop's enigmatic reputation. Not that anyone's complaining. Bees and barn owls make use of deserted hamerkop nests, and it is not unusual to find Egyptian geese, ducks and even the odd giant eagle-owl squatting on the roof.

In some African tribal cultures the hamerkop is identified with Impundulu, the Lightning Bird, a mythical creature that is visible only to women and – how can I put this – people who are not men. Thunder is caused by the Lightning Bird flapping its wings, and a bolt of lightning is a sure indicator that the bird has descended to earth to lay its eggs. If you're daring, you can dig up the eggs at the site of a lightning strike. Ground into powder and mixed with a fish that shines in the dark and other items not available at your local supermarket, you can use the resultant potion to ensure that anyone you don't like gets blasted to bits with a trillion volts.

The Khoikhoi believed that the hamerkop could see the future reflected in the mirrored surface of a pond and consequently regarded the bird with great awe and respect and not a little trepidation. If one of the birds flew up to a Khoikhoi dwelling and emitted three sharp cries, the occupants could be reasonably certain that it had foreseen the imminent demise of one of their number. Everyone then just had to wait, fidgeting nervously, for the sight of a falling star, the immediate precursor of death. When this duly appeared, the hamerkop would fly around the roof of the dwelling emitting its plaintive cry.

Certainly the humble hamerkop, preoccupied with real estate development, theatrical productions and fishing trips, is unaware of its mystical status. Perhaps the real magic lies in the effect this otherwise drab bird has on our imaginations, something that has undoubtedly helped ensure that it is left in peace.

HIPPO

One of the most popular small statues kept in homes in Ancient Egypt had the head of a hippo, enormous breasts and the stomach of a pregnant woman. The deity's name was Tawaret, and it was believed that she protected pregnant women, mothers and small children. Paradoxically, Tawaret was the consort of Set the Destroyer, the Egyptian god of death and evil, an intimidating figure whose gloomy image seldom joined his wife's on the domestic mantelpiece.

The Ancient Egyptians shared the River Nile and its banks with hippos, and this brief glimpse into their complicated cosmology shows that they had a good understanding of the dichotomous nature of their bulky neighbours.

Hippos make exemplary mothers, but they are also credited with killing and maiming more human beings in Africa than any other animal. The reason is not that hard to find. No other large wild animal in modern times habitually lives in such close proximity to human settlements. Human beings, like hippos, need water in rivers, dams or lakes to survive, and most attacks occur on or near the water's edge in poor rural communities that don't have access to piped water. Attacks, most of which take place at night while hippos are out grazing, seldom seem to be provoked, though the highly territorial hippo probably has a different take on this.

Hippo attacks in Africa are often met with a fatalism that doesn't accompany attacks by other wild animals such as snakes, lions and elephants. 'Villagers defend crime-fighting hippo' bellowed the headline of a South African newspaper in 2002. It reported that a young man rolling home at night from a soccer match had been attacked and severely injured by a hippo. Conservation officials considered shooting the offender, but the local chief would have none of that. He insisted that the hippo be relocated, a sentiment vociferously echoed by other villagers. They pointed out that the presence of hippos patrolling the environs of the village each night kept burglars and muggers at bay.

Other wild animals are often viewed as intruders, but the hippo seems to be regarded as a cranky neighbour, the type who grumpily nods hello across the garden fence, but woe betide you if you set foot on his newly mowed lawn.

Hippos are very good at mowing lawns. The vast bulk of their diet is grass, and, if necessary, they will travel a long way to find it – 20 kilometres and more being an unexceptional nightly excursion. Where possible though, they stay close to their home stretch of water, be it a river or dam, nocturnally munching along the banks to a distance of 2 or 3 kilometres and cropping the grass with their big lips to create lawns that the Palm Beach Country Club would be proud of.

A typical hippo day resembles one that most of us dream about while we're stuck in traffic on a Monday morning: water, beach and piña coladas. In consequence they have a reputation for indolence, reinforced by the fact that every single one of them looks like a prime candidate for a Weight Watchers course. It's unfair of course; life for a hippo is far from an endless round of water sports, pigging out and snoozing.

Hippo bulls lead a particularly dangerous lifestyle, routinely suffering ghastly injuries and even losing their lives in regular battles to secure or defend their watery domain and harem, two of life's chores that routinely go hand in hand. Young males are driven away by the dominant bull when they reach five or six years old, and it is no easy thing to find alternative accommodation, especially when there are equally cantankerous and belligerent neighbours upstream and downstream.

Making it out of infancy is a perilous journey in itself. Pregnant females leave the herd to find a secluded spot when ready to give birth, but a mere two weeks later it's time to introduce junior to his plump cousins, uncles and aunts and, of course, the big enchilada himself. If after the first sniff the dominant bull suspects infidelity, or maybe just because he's in one of his moods, he will attack the baby. If this occurs the mother justifies her reputation among the Egyptians as Tawaret, aggressively keeping the male at bay, often supported in her unequal task by other females. Even if dad does give his nod of approval, it isn't all beer and skittles for the cute young butterball. Crocodiles and lions are an ever-present menace.

Despite their bursts of ferocity and the impressive human body count they manage to rack up each year, hippos generally have a benign and cuddly reputation, at least from the safe perspective of city dwellers. The legendary wanderer, Huberta the Hippo, subject of many a gooey children's story, helped in the creation of this sentimental perspective. Starting out as Hubert until she flashed her eyelashes and showed a bit of shapely thigh, Huberta made an epic journey down the east coast of South Africa from Lake St Lucia to the vicinity of King William's Town. She moved from pool to pool and river to river, taking four years over the trip, never hurting or threatening anyone. In the process she became a darling of the press, and there was much despairing beating of editors' chests when she met her end in the Keiskamma River, shot by hunters unaware of her celebrity status.

More recently, video footage of a hippo rescuing an impala from the jaws of a crocodile, nuzzling the hapless, half-dead creature and seemingly trying to help it to its feet, has helped reinforce the hippo's benevolent image. Other, similar rescues have been recorded and zoologists have yet to come up with a plausible explanation.

Perhaps the Great Spirit knows. African legend at least has a theory to explain why hippos disperse their droppings both in the water and on land by vigorously wagging their stubby tails. In the beginning, the Great Spirit allowed hippos to live both on land and in the water, but he was worried that with their cavernous mouths and huge appetites they would soon eat all the fish. He therefore extracted a promise that they would eat only grass and, to ensure they complied, commanded that they scatter their dung so that he could see at a glance if it contained fish bones.

The Romans gave the hippopotamus its name, which in Latin means 'river horse', a description adopted from the Ancient Greeks. In Afrikaans it is known as a *seekoei*, which translates as 'sea cow'. Both names bestow an improbable domesticity on a creature that, in the wrong set of circumstances, can bite a person in half.

KLIPSPRINGER

If the last 200 million years have taught us anything, it's that extreme specialization is a risky strategy. Creatures that didn't want to listen have gone the way of the dodo, a bird that started out as a pigeon on a holiday to Mauritius and ended up as a kind of flightless Billy Bunter with a silly beak. If it had stayed a pigeon it might have avoided meeting its demise in common sailors' cooking pots and, ironically, could even now be perched instead on Admiral Nelson's head in Trafalgar Square, attending to its private business.

The diminutive klipspringer has also failed to heed the lesson, but, remarkably, its strategy seems to have paid off, at least for the time being. Africa's vast spaces are littered with rocky outcrops, islands of a sort in an enormous sea of woodland, scrub and savanna. By a lucky happenstance many such outcrops are located in game reserves, and the small antelopes cling tenaciously to them like life rafts. Barring bush fires, a pair of klipspringers might spend their entire lives on the same pile of boulders, a finite world usually encompassing a mere 20 to 30 hectares, and sometimes a lot less.

Adapting to a life on the rocks has meant making major changes, beginning with the hooves. Klipspringers stand on the hard tips of their rounded hooves, which have undergone a complicated transformation and are unlike those of any other antelope. This radical adaptation enables them to get a sure purchase. Helped along by powerful hindquarters, they can effortlessly outrun, outjump and outmanoeuvre virtually any predator in their rocky home range. On the earth and soft sands in between outcrops, such specialized hooves are not, of course, such a hot innovation, which helps explain why the animals are committed homebodies.

Even the most accomplished acrobats sometimes slip and fall, which is something you really don't want to do on granite rocks. The klipspringer has taken the necessary precautions, evolving a thick, springy coat made up of hollow, coarse hair that helps cushion the impact if it gets too cocky and takes a rare tumble. An added bonus is that the coat provides effective insulation when the cold winter wind whistles through the klipspringer's craggy home.

Unlike other antelopes, with their complicated harems and all the bickering and social upheaval that this inevitably entails, klipspringers are monogamous. Once hitched, they stay together for life and, in a seemingly touching display of mutual devotion, rarely stray more than a few dozen metres from each other. Only the worst kind of cynic would suggest that if you're stuck on a rock in the middle of nowhere there really aren't many other places to be.

They take turns feeding and keeping watch, occasionally taking time out to mark their territory by inserting the tip of a twig into a prominent scent gland beside their eyes. The female goes first, and the male follows, dabbing the same twig with a sticky potion and licking it to release the aroma as if in affirmation of their undying bond.

The male further displays his gallantry by taking less time eating and longer spells on watch, and especially so when junior comes along. Raising young is an anxious time for klipspringers and no picnic for the infant, which spends the first three months of its life lying flat in a sheltered crevice, hiding from raptors and other potential dangers. The young are weaned at about four months and usually leave home after a year. There is some debate as to whether they are forced out or can't wait to get away from parental control. As in our own case, both probably happen. Female offspring are more likely to remain for a while, amid scandalous rumours of incest.

Secure on the top of a favourite boulder and supremely confident in their rock-bounding abilities, a klipspringer pair sometimes likes to cock a snook at approaching predators. When they spot a threat, typically a leopard or a hyena, both male and female stand their ground and remain in view, giving a short cry that has been likened to the blast from a toy trumpet. This lets the predator know that it's been spotted and, with the element of surprise gone, saves everyone a lot of unnecessary effort. Klipspringers tended to be easy targets for hunters with rifles precisely because of this behaviour, and in the hunt-happy days of yore many ended up donating their well-cushioned coats to be used as saddle stuffing.

When all is said and done, perhaps the klipspringer has its own lesson to impart after all: if you find your perfect niche, maybe it's best to stick with it. Kicking off your shoes or throwing your flight feathers to the four corners of the wind on an idyllic tropical island may seem a good idea, but you can never really know who or what may one day come sailing up over the horizon.

SPOTTED HYENA

If, by some bizarre quirk of fate, you found yourself acting as a public relations consultant for a pack of hyenas, it would be best to insist on payment in advance; yes, payment in advance, maybe a tooth-proof vest and a guaranteed place in the witness protection programme.

Spotted hyenas have never made much of an effort to get along with anyone, even each other. The word 'popular' doesn't feature in their lexicon, and they don't seem to give a hoot about their image, often cackling with hysterical laughter when some other animal takes a tumble and gets dismembered in the bush.

Big-game hunters in the first half of the 20th century regarded them as barely worth a bullet. They were cowardly, shifty reprobates who made a living by butchering the sick and helpless and scavenging rotten leftovers. They could always be found hanging around the tables of other noble and bullet-worthy carnivores, typically lions and leopards, or otherwise outside a safari tent looking for an opportunity to steal stuff.

The first dent in their implacably evil reputation was made in Tanzania's Ngorongoro Crater in the 1970s. Research revealed that hyenas surrounding a pride of lions as they dined imperiously on a zebra carcass might not be the riffraff we'd always supposed. It turned out that more often than not, at least in the Ngorongoro, the carcass belonged to the hyenas – they had hunted and killed the hapless zebra during the night. The lions were the robbers and then had the gall to put on a breakfast show for camera-wielding tourists. All those happy snaps were taken under false pretences.

If hyenas are aware of this cautious and subtle shift in public opinion they don't seem to have taken much notice, presumably because the revelation is nothing new as far as they're concerned. They still live their nocturnal lives, doing the nefarious things they've always done. That includes eating people when the opportunity presents itself. The corpse-strewn battlefields in the horn of Africa have lately provided a bonanza for spotted hyenas, so much so that they are now taking more of an interest in live bipedal specimens. In Malawi, they have a long record of chomping humans, particularly during the hot season when it's cooler to sleep outside. In the rest of rural Africa such incidents are almost certainly underreported.

The fact that hyenas don't get the same publicity as other man-eaters is probably because we don't like to admit to the idea. It's one thing being gobbled by an awesome great white shark or chewed by the king of beasts, but a skulking, cowardly hyena? Another reason, to be fair, is that killing human beings is not something hyenas really do that often. If you choose to believe everything else about them, the one thing worth admitting is that their risk-assessment skills are second to none. Killing and eating humans who have access to guns and tend to form outraged mobs is a decidedly risky business.

Hyenas evolved, at least in part, to cash in on the fact that the other major predators are wasteful eaters. A lion typically consumes only about 60% of a carcass, leaving plenty of marrow-filled bones and other bits and pieces. Hyenas' jaws and titanium teeth are able to exert immense pressure, enough to crack open and break apart even the largest bones. That done, their digestive juices are so potent that they can efficiently process virtually any organic matter, including bones, hooves, hides and even horns, thereby extracting the last ounce of nourishment from even the bleakest pile of animal remains. They're not bothered about medals, but cleaning up the landscape should at least earn them some brownie points with the environmental lobby.

The benefit of eating things that are dead already is that you don't have to risk life and limb tackling something that might fight back. Even the most innocuous-looking quadruped can sometimes land a devastating kick or may stick its horns into all the wrong places. Nor do you have to expend energy chasing after fleet-footed meals. Unless it's absolutely necessary, you can leave that to the glitzy superstars. When they've done what's required it's just a matter of hanging around or, in the case of leopards, scaring them up a tree and waiting for bits to fall. With any luck, the whole carcass drops in your lap. When it comes to stealing kills, cheetahs are a bit of a joke as far as hyenas are concerned. Unfortunately there aren't that many of them, and sometimes, like it or not, you just have to do your own dirty work and hope that the local lions don't switch roles with you.

To the casual observer the social life of spotted hyenas is something of a shambles. It's not always clear who's who, who belongs to which gang, whether there even is a gang, or if they're just a lot of layabouts with shifting mutual interests. They can be found alone or in packs of anything up to 60 or 70 individuals. Even a communal hunt doesn't seem to be pre-planned but rather a question of joining in on an individual initiative.

Female hyenas are big, butch and scary as far as the browbeaten males are concerned. Even an adolescent female can see off all but the largest and most dominant males. They are pumped up with so much testosterone that confusing things have happened to the female genitalia, which, at a glance, look just like a male's you-know-what. As a result, for a long while hyenas were thought to be hermaphrodite, yet another thing to add to their weirdo image.

Hyena cubs are born in an underground den with fully functioning canines that they invariably put to good use despatching siblings of the same sex, the only mammal known to do this. Mothers usually give birth to twins, so if you pop out as a male you have to keep your paws crossed that you have a sister not a brother, or vice versa. The statistical result is that about 25 per cent of hyena pups never get to see the light of day.

If you set out to create an image as the most obnoxious kid on the block, you couldn't do a better job than the hyena, nature's newest type of carnivore. But then again, who will blame us for trying? As we bomb, shoot and rapaciously consume our way towards extinction, they may yet have the last laugh.

SECRETARYBIRD

A mong its many other esoteric distinctions, the secretarybird is a favourite of postal authorities around the world and has featured on more stamps than most other birds. It has pride of place in the coat of arms of South Africa and is the national symbol of Sudan. Its image is also used in the logo of the Malaysian Association of the Institute of Chartered Secretaries and Administrators, symbolizing professionalism and high moral standards. Although the secretarybird is totally absent from Asia, this honour is presumably inspired by the bird's reputation for never cooking the books and going straight home to its mate each night.

The secretarybird purportedly got its strange name because the black feathers sticking out of the back of its head reminded Victorian observers of office clerks, who would habitually put quill pens behind their ears when turning the pages of their ponderous ledgers. Another and more plausible theory suggests that the name actually derives from an Arabic word meaning 'hunter bird', which sounds very similar to the French *secretaire*. Whatever the origin, we're stuck with it. Given a choice, and assuming it mattered, the bird would probably prefer to be known by its other, less used but more accurate colloquial name: the marching eagle.

Although assigned to its own distinct family, *Sagittarius serpentarius* is in effect an eagle on stilts, replete with beak and talons. It is superbly adapted for a life on the open veld and can surely be thankful, despite the name, that it's not stuck in a stuffy office with a boss continually making inappropriate remarks and trying to ruffle its feathers. Its association with serpents derives from the fact that when it finds a snake it stamps the stuffing out of it, its feet and claws exerting a force that could break your hand.

This dramatic routine earned it the respect of many snake-fearing African communities and in consequence it was largely left alone.

Depending upon their availability, snakes usually form a relatively small part of the bird's diet, though the secretarybird will always enjoy them when it can – fat or thin, big or small. It swallows small snakes whole, but larger specimens are torn to pieces with the bill. Although well protected by its feathers, it's not immune to snake venom and takes due care to ensure that the object of its merciless stamping is well and truly dead before feeding. On rare occasions this entails hoisting the snake into the air and dropping it from a great height, a method employed by bearded vultures to crack tortoise shells. On a humdrum day the bird selects from a standard menu that includes insects, lizards, mice, chameleons, locusts and other invertebrates. There have been reported cases of secretarybirds preying on cheetah cubs and other infant mammals when the opportunity presents itself.

The birds are endemic to Africa, living on open grasslands from the fringes of the Sahara Desert to the Cape of Good Hope, as far away from an office as possible. Given their lifestyle they shun forests, thickly wooded areas and mountainous regions. In keeping with their black-and-grey air of official gravitas they are largely silent, occasionally uttering a guttural croak.

The birds are committed to a terrestrial lifestyle, covering several kilometres a day at a steady pace. They pause every now and again to stamp on the ground, wings outstretched, to cause a local commotion and flush out the edible inhabitants of the long grass. When threatened itself, the secretarybird runs at first, often with partially opened wings; only if that's not enough to elude a determined pursuer does it finally take to the air. These birds can fly very well, resembling storks rather than eagles in flight, and have been observed riding thermals to heights of 3,000 metres and more. To keep fit, or more probably to advertise their presence to others of their species, they fly around their territory before settling down for the night.

True to their imagined Victorian values, male and female often keep a respectable distance from each other while they're out walking in the veld and thus often appear to be alone. By contrast, their mating displays throw decorum to the wind and are exceptionally flamboyant. Male and female soar in wide circles, swoop and plunge towards earth, sometimes clasping each other's talons like two mutually besotted skydivers.

The birds generally pair for life and build a nest together near the top of a tree, preferring the flat top of an acacia, but making do with other types of tree or even a tall bush where necessary. The important thing is that the nest be impregnable from below, which it invariably is, and hence very difficult to spot from the ground. The flip side is that it's visible from the air, and the chicks are sometimes targeted by other raptors if both parents are absent. The birds are remarkably faithful to their nest, returning to roost at night even when no eggs or chicks are present. The flat bundle of sticks grows year by year in the manner of an eagle's eyrie and can eventually expand to a diameter of nearly 3 metres – more commodious than the average office cubicle.

A female lays two, and often three, eggs. They hatch at short intervals, as incubation begins with the first egg. A consequence of this is that the last chick to see daylight usually dies of starvation, being unable to compete with its slightly larger siblings. The young birds can fly after about 80 days, but they often leave the nest to strut their stuff a few days before they're able to take to the air. When that day finally comes, the young birds clear their desks and leave the building, living a nomadic existence until, hopefully, they find a mate.

AFRICAN CLAWLESS OTTER

If you drop dead and it turns out you have to be reincarnated, maybe choose to come back as an otter, especially if you enjoy water sports, fish and crustaceans. Of all the animals struggling to get some modest pleasure out of life, including us dumb nuts, otters seem to have it made. They are top of the food chain in their semi-aquatic wonderworld, and can eat 15 per cent of their body weight every day and still keep fit and trim – you try tucking in to six or seven kilograms of your favourite foods and see what happens.

What's more, they are so well adapted to their eco-niche that they don't have to spend the whole damned day at the office trying to put food on the table. They are intelligent animals, and there's plenty of time for high jinks or just plain lounging around. If you were an otter in the Tsitsikamma you could lie on a rock, concealed in the shade, maybe munching a crab, and watch human hikers puffing and panting against the clock with their 50-kilogram packs on the – wait for it – Otter Trail. I'll leave you to work out who's got the best plan.

All you need to be a happy otter is a lake or running river, preferably one that doesn't have *Homo sapiens* dumping chemicals and effluent upstream. You'd want it to be well stocked with crabs,

frogs, molluscs and fish, and, as a bonus, you may even be able to live near a river mouth, take the odd dip in the surf, or potter about on the smorgasbord of the intertidal zone. At least for now, the southern and western stretches of coast in South Africa are ideal and relatively pristine, with many river estuaries.

Further north, given the pressure of human populations, things aren't so rosy. That said, the otter is still comfortably on the least endangered list and ranges through most of Africa south of the Sahara, pretty much wherever there is permanent water and bush, with the notable exception of the Congo Basin and the arid areas of Namibia, Botswana and the Northern Cape. The otters as a whole are represented on every continent except Antarctica.

African clawless otters (a.k.a. Cape clawless otters) are members of the weasel family (Mustelidae) and have the same bright-eyed curiosity as their cousins. They are closely related to badgers and distantly related – though it's probably not something they brag about – to skunks. Unlike their terrestrial cousins, otters are relatively slow and clumsy on land but consummate acrobats in water, propelled along like flexible torpedoes by their powerful tails and partially webbed hind feet. They are more than a match for a mullet. Clawless forepaws are ideal for digging in the sediment and flipping rocks and logs in search of hidden molluscs, worms, crabs and other otter delicacies. They take larger prey to dry land for consumption but do have the endearing and comical habit of occasionally snacking on manageable foods while casually floating on their backs.

Otters are territorial and, by and large, live a solitary life, usually only venturing onto neighbouring ranges to find a mate. Home is an underground burrow in an overgrown riverbank, known as a holt, which allows easy access to the aquatic hunting ground and a safe haven if something nasty comes along. Otters have few natural predators, the main ones being pythons and crocodiles, where these creatures occur – another good reason to opt for the southern Cape coast. As usual, among the biggest threats are our rapacious ways.

Deforestation in river catchments poses a particularly serious threat to the otter's wellbeing, resulting as it does in erosion and increased turbidity, which, in turn, impacts on fish populations, not to mention making it difficult to see prey under water.

December is otter mating season, and once the slap and tickle is over, male (boar) and female (sow) go their separate ways, the female predictably being lumbered with raising the pups. The young are weaned in a couple of months, reach maturity after a year and are then booted out to find their own way in the world. An otter pup can be almost as long as its mother, and, if they are seen frolicking together, they may be mistaken for a couple.

Adults reach an average of 140 centimetres in overall length, one-third of which is tail, and they tip the scales at anything between 12 and 21 kilograms. Their lifespan in the wild is about 10 years, but this can double in the dubious comforts of captivity. They have little or no body fat, despite that relatively large food intake, and rely on their thick, smooth fur, particularly silky on their underbellies, to provide effective insulation in cold water. Although fond of sunbathing, they avoid the midday African heat by spending much of the day in a shady retreat, or in their holt, only venturing out at night and in the cool of morning and evening. In heavily populated or semi-urban areas they tend to be entirely nocturnal, and who can blame them?

PRAYING
MANTIS

Not many bugs can claim to be a martial arts instructor, a pest controller, a demigod and a prophet, but the mantis takes such job descriptions and accolades in its stride.

While the Ancient Greeks were philosophically concluding that the inscrutable insect was contemplating something a great deal more profound than its next lunch, their Chinese counterparts were busy writing poems about its courage and fearlessness. Meanwhile, down south, the San (Bushmen) passed on strange and occasionally comical cosmological tales in which the mantis was the dashing hero. The rest of us think it's praying, which it probably is, but only for the next fat moth or grasshopper to come a little closer.

There are about 2,000 members of the insect order Mantodea, of which about 120 can be found in southern Africa, the rest being spread out over the whole vast compass of the earth, with the exception of Antarctica. They come in a weird variety of shapes and sizes, adapted to look like leaves, twigs, bark, flowers and grass, depending upon their habitat. The variant most of us are familiar with is the green mantis, the one that flies through the window at night, lands on your pillow and then looks you up and down as though it's you who's in the wrong bed.

The mantis can move its triangular head and large compound eyes to look up and down and side to side and even – as you jump from the covers and bolt for the door – over its shoulder. No other insect can do this, and that's enough to freak out all but the most dedicated entomomaniac.

The evolutionary point of this aptitude is not just to give you the heebie-jeebies. It enables the mantis to remain absolutely motionless while it discreetly inspects it environs for meals and potential threats. There wouldn't otherwise be much point in investing in all that complicated camouflage. Mantises are ambush predators, and the point of an ambush is of course to remain undetected until it's time to strike. The mantis that comes through your window seems to have forgotten this or, more likely, has been disorientated by the bedside light. Mantises hunt by sight and are hence diurnal, but if all those punch-drunk bugs want to knock themselves senseless clattering around an artificial mini-sun, why wait until morning?

Mantids like their food fresh and in fact won't eat anything that isn't still alive and kicking. They usually start at the head, thus ensuring that there is no backchat during dinner. They are voracious eaters and polish off even quite substantial bugs in record time. Prey is captured with a rapid strike of the raptorial forelegs, a movement too fast for the human eye to follow and one that particularly impressed the Chinese martial arts aficionados. The forelegs are lined with tooth-like spikes to ensure that the victim's escape is well-nigh impossible.

Staples of mantids' diets include moths, beetles, butterflies, flies, grasshoppers and almost every other kind of insect, including many that we regards as pests. Large species of mantid, which hopefully live in the Twilight Zone, have been known to take on small lizards, birds and even rodents.

The fact that they eat insect pests has helped pump up their image as green crusaders and led to a fairly brisk trade in young mantises, the principal customers being organic gardeners who eschew the use of pesticides. When eagerly released in its new home the undiscerning mantis is equally happy to chomp its way through the local population of benevolent bugs, but this detail tends to get lost in the eco-wash.

When it's time to mate, the much smaller male shows little sign of ambivalence towards the upcoming nuptials, despite the very real possibility that he might literally be consumed by passion. Instances of the female mantis starting to eat her mate during the act of copulation are well documented, though probably exaggerated. When she does, she starts with his head, which has little effect on her lover's performance and, if anything, urges what's left of him to try even harder. This bizarre behaviour has not escaped the attention of extreme feminists, to whom the female mantis has become something of a totem.

As befits an insect of such obvious accomplishments, the egg-laying process is a fairly high-tech affair. The female first sprays a ball of sticky foam, usually onto the underside of a leaf, and then prepares individual chambers in it for each egg. Once in, the eggs are secured by a kind of tiny valve. She has to work rapidly, as the foam soon hardens when exposed to air. Remarkably, all this is achieved with the tip of her tail and her hind legs so it's little wonder that she needs to be able to look over her shoulder.

WARTHOG

The first warthog was a handsome pig according to African folklore. So much so that he grew narcissistic and arrogant and took perverse pleasure in insulting every animal he came across while trotting about on the African stage. He eventually took things too far by insulting a particularly large lion. To escape the lion's wrath, the warthog plunged head first into an aardvark hole in which a porcupine was having a quiet snooze and promptly got a face full of quills. Unsurprisingly he could find no one willing to help pull them out and was forced to do it himself, so becoming disfigured. Since then he's been pug ugly and only able to land character parts.

Not that this has obstructed a dazzling career. Few people on the planet are unaware of the warthog, at least in his persona as Pumbaa in *The Lion King*, a blockbuster film in which he plays a kind of comical retired sergeant major. His close friend and confidant is played by a wisecracking meerkat. In real life, resting warthogs have been observed allowing banded mongooses to groom them looking for ticks, showing that fact can be just as cute as fiction.

Warthogs are perennials of Africa's savannas and, being diurnal, are invariably seen during a trip to a game reserve, even when all the other prima donnas stay obstinately hidden in the wings. They have a comedy routine that involves running away in single file with their tails stuck up like radio antennas. It may not sound like much, but it usually gets the audience smiling.

Warthogs run away a lot. Apart from lions (presumably still fuming about that ancestral insult), adult warthogs have to run away from a full cast of other villains including leopards, wild dogs, cheetahs and spotted hyenas. Their young also fall prey to Verreaux's eagles, pythons and jackals. When pursued, warthogs head straight for the nearest aardvark burrow, one of several such bolt holes dotted about their home range, all of which have been thoroughly checked out for hidden porcupines. The young dive straight in, but most adult warthogs slam into reverse at the last minute and enter backwards to put their tusks and their best face forward.

Beauty is in the eye of the beholder, as the saying goes, but maybe it's as well to remember that during life's auditions the beholder is usually having a derogatory snigger behind everyone's back, not just the warthog's. It must be bad enough having a face to sink a thousand ships, without also having to make your way in the world saddled with such an offensive name. Everyone immediately homes in on the facial warts, but they are not really warts at all, not in the warty witch sense; they're bony protuberances. They're there to protect the eyes during battles with other boars to see who gets to play on centre stage and land the plum part with the leading lady.

Looks aside, boars can really turn on the charm when it comes to courting, sniffing around everyone's aardvark hole to see who's in the mood. When they get lucky, they approach the object of their desire with a jaunty walk, swinging their hips, tail held high, chomping their jaws, grunting and drooling profusely. If that sounds a tad unromantic, maybe you have to be there, ideally as a female warthog.

A bit over five months later the piglets are born, usually three or four in a litter but sometimes as many as eight. Birth takes place at the onset of the rainy season, which heralds the appearance of new grass, but as usual in nature, there is inevitably a trade-off; the downside is the rain itself, which can come down in buckets and flood the family hole. To avoid this potential catastrophe, the mother immediately shoves the little pigs up onto a kind of pre-prepared mantelpiece, like a row of trophies, just in case. A week later they are up and out in the open, enjoying the grass, and begin little sparring matches to establish who's who in matters pertaining to the order for suckling and trotting behind mum.

Rather unnecessarily, given that the grass is often bigger than they are, very young warthogs get down on their front knees to feed, just like their parents. Anatomically speaking they are actually bending their wrists, but we don't have to be pedantic about it. You could be forgiven for thinking that they're taking a bow, maybe acknowledging the silent applause that accompanies a performance in survival that has lasted millions of years.

ELAND

During the long, slow plod of evolution every species has to make choices. Some of us turn out sleek and sexy, while others get into an indecisive muddle and, like the platypus and the aardvark, end up looking rather ridiculous. The antelope are no exception. There are curvaceous sports models, such as the springbok and impala, or the dashing sable with it scimitar horns, and then there's the eland. What on earth was it thinking when it put that little head on top of such a humongous body?

Then again, looks aren't everything, and the eland does somehow still manage to exude an air of ponderous gravitas, complete with dewlap, a bit like a Brahman bull.

Finding itself surrounded by carnivores with the latest and greatest in predatory equipment, the eland seems to have surreptitiously torn a leaf from the *Diplodocus* handbook and opted for bulk. It's a pity about the head, but, as the dinosaurs discovered, when trying to keep up with current trends you can't always get everything just right.

The upside of being hefty is that most carnivores, even the big ones, take one look and decide it's probably not worth the effort. Bulking up might mean that you end up being the slowest antelope around, 40 kilometres per hour flat out compared with the springbok's 88 kilometres per hour, but some carnivores are keen on fast food anyway. Cheetahs can get to the head of the queue by belting along at well over 100 kilometres per hour, and wild dogs are prepared to trot behind remorselessly until even the fleetest buck finally runs out of gas. With its cruise control set at about 22 kilometres per hour, the eland can go on forever.

The downside of having a big body is having to eat and eat, then eat some more. Eland are among the least choosy of the antelope when it comes to what they tuck away, being both browsers and grazers: grass, leaves, twigs, fruits, seeds and pods, tubers – bring it on with second helpings. Location is also not that big an issue, and they are equally at home in grasslansd, acacia savanna, semi-desert habitat and mountain slopes up to a height of about 4,500 metres. Their bones have even been found more than halfway up Kilimanjaro, but maybe that was a case of taking a lunch too far. What they don't like are swamps, forest and true desert.

When it was getting kitted out the one big problem the eland could never foresee was men with rifles. If you're as big as a barn door and not very fast, you make an easy target. Now that the cordite smoke has cleared the result is balefully obvious, particularly in South Africa. Add the fact that eland are especially susceptible to rinderpest, and it's a relief to find any left at all. Having survived the great slaughter, the few that do remain in the wild are understandably skittish and seldom seen. They purportedly have the longest flight distance of any South African mammal, moving off if a person or a vehicle approaches closer than about 400–500 metres.

The San revered the mighty eland not just as a walking mountain of prime steaks, but as a mystic fellow traveller. The creator god Kaggen's first child was an eland, and he was understandably very fond of it. He chose to manifest himself as one of the great antelope when the mood took him, or perhaps when his praying mantis disguise got a little tight around the middle.

The eland was the central figure in several San rites of passage, including the often difficult and perplexing transition to manhood. Successfully hunting a beast that weighs 20 times as much as you do, using only a dinky bow and arrow, is the stuff of tribal legend. Providing enough meat to feed the family and all the friends and relations for a long, long time was guaranteed to make you popular, not to mention man of the month.

Representations of eland feature prominently in San rock art, painted with a soul-stretching intimacy and sensitivity that clearly shows the pivotal part they must have played in the spiritual and corporeal lives of the artists. The diminutive men and their brushes and paints are long gone, but the art endures, often in secret rocky places where the eland itself still walks, but as a ghost.

CROW

The Norse god Odin had a crow perched on each shoulder, one called Thought and the other Desire. He would send them out each morning to ask questions of the living and the dead, and in this way always knew what was going on. What was routinely going on, at least in the Viking world, was pillaging and bloodshed.

Throughout history, crows could be relied upon to turn up for a public execution and were always the first to arrive to help clean up the carnage on battlefields, the eyes of the slain being a favoured delicacy. A gathering of crows was called a 'murder', and they inevitably came to be closely associated with death, a reputation helped along by the fact that they were always dressed for the occasion in funereal black.

Crows worked out long ago that human beings are good at killing, not only each other, but just about everything else that flies, crawls or walks. They also observed that we're not always so great at cleaning up the mess afterwards. Keeping up with modern trends, local crows spend a good deal of time patrolling the highways and byways of South Africa, feasting on the birds, mammals and reptiles that have prematurely met their maker under speeding trucks and cars. So bounteous and predictable is this macabre meals-under-wheels service that many now nest on top of convenient roadside telegraph poles. Thanks to their quick wits, they are rarely numbered among the casualties themselves.

South Africa's home-grown family of crows has three members: the pied, the black crow and the white-necked raven, the last-mentioned being by far the largest. Their range extends over almost the entire country, though the raven usually prefers to remain fairly aloof in mountainous terrain, periodically adding to its dodgy reputation as a thug by raiding chicken runs or attacking lambs and disabled sheep. The others make a living wherever opportunities present themselves, from the countryside to suburbia. They will eat just about anything. A piece of rare fillet is preferred, but if there's only an overripe banana available, that will do.

All crows are credited with considerable intelligence and excellent memories. Aesop told a fable of a thirsty crow dropping pebbles into a jug of water until the level rose high enough to enable it to drink, thus demonstrating a profound knowledge of the laws of displacement. If you think Aesop was just into tall tales, consider the sobering fact that a similar modern experiment with real crows produced exactly the same result.

Wild crows also seem to have the unnerving ability to recognize individual human faces, notably those of people they can't stand. A conservation official in Durban charged with exterminating a municipal plague of the immigrant house crow, *Corvus splendens*, soon found himself living in a kind of endless sequel to Alfred

Hitchcock's film *The Birds*. Given the crows' wily ways, all his attempts at reducing their numbers met with dismal failure, but even out of uniform, walking in a crowd on the street or innocently paddling a canoe on the river, the crows recognized him and let him know of their undying enmity. What was particularly unsettling was that all the crows in the city reacted in the same way, wherever he was, despite the fact that his extermination attempts had been restricted to a few specific locations.

Rather like the Mafia, crows are big on family. Most are social by nature, and interaction with their own kind seems very important to them, particularly for the young and unattached. They usually pair for life, and when breeding time rolls round, juveniles from the previous year sometimes help their parents gather nesting material. Thereafter, both parents take turns incubating the eggs and caring for the chicks.

Like the Mafia, they also purportedly hold their own courts, presumably to try transgressors of the crow code. Weird assemblies of crows have been observed at various times and places forming a circle around one of their luckless peers. The croaking and crowing continues for some considerable time, and then suddenly, as if on a given signal, all the members of the assembly pounce on the individual in the centre and peck him to death. They then disperse and fly away.

'Once upon a midnight dreary' begins Edgar Allen Poe's poem *The Raven*, and it doesn't get much more cheerful than that.

MALACHITE KINGFISHER

When popular King Ceyx of Ancient Greece fell into the sea and drowned in circumstances that have never been fully explained, the gods of Olympus were mighty upset. They promptly arranged for him and his wife Halcyon to be reincarnated as kingfishers and made a floating nest for the happy couple out of fish bones. Whether Queen Halcyon was quite ready for this domestic rearrangement is a moot point. Be that as it may, the gods have always made sure that the weather is calm when the couple are on their waterborne nest. This helps explain why an old name for the kingfisher was the halcyon and also why seafarers still refer to halcyon days when describing periods of calm on the ocean.

Well-meaning old gods aside, there are 10 species of kingfisher in southern Africa and none of them, with the occasional exception of the giant and the pied kingfishers, fish in the sea. Six of them don't eat fish at all.

The malachite kingfisher is one of the smallest and eats very small freshwater fish, crustaceans and aquatic insects. It has also been observed catching dragonflies in flight, which, if you've tried it, you'll know is no mean feat. The malachite is fairly common throughout South Africa, wherever there are rivers, streams and marshes, though it especially favours the halcyon waters of dams and pans. It also turns up on temporary stretches of water that may dry out in winter, relying for its meals on the little seasonal fish that miraculously and bizarrely appear each year from drought-resistant eggs.

At an overall length of about 14 centimetres and weighing next to nothing, the malachite can perch unperturbed on grass stems and slender reeds and is notoriously difficult to spot. It usually takes up position about 1–1.5 metres above the water, dashing away over the surface on blurred wings when disturbed. Like most other kingfishers it bobs its head up and down when seated on its perch, and this can give its position away to the eagle-eyed observer.

In appearance the malachite is very similar to the pygmy kingfisher, and I solemnly promise that you won't get into trouble if you mistake the one for the other. Both are about the same size, although the pygmy is very slightly shorter and broader; both have a red beak and both are mainly an iridescent blue with light brown underparts and white throats. You will have to get out your bird book to work out the differences, mainly in the shape of the head, but the similarity ends with appearance. The pygmy is a seasonal visitor to South Africa, arriving from its winter condo in Central Africa in October and departing again in March or April. During this period it is fairly common along the KwaZulu-Natal coast, ranging inland up to an altitude of about 1,000 metres. Unlike the malachite, it is exclusively an insectivore and does not fish, inhabiting thick woodland, forest edges and clearings.

If you were just beginning to get comfortable with these differences, I'm sorry to point out that the malachite is also very similar to the half-collared kingfisher, another permanent resident. I won't give you a headache by going into details – suffice it to say that the half-collared's beak is very definitely black, and it is a bigger bird, about 19 centimetres in length.

Like many of its relatives, the malachite nests in burrows in riverbanks composed of sandy or clay soils, usually less than 3 metres above the water surface. Both male and female share the heavy-duty task of excavating the tunnel, which can be up to 90 centimetres long, ending in an enlarged nesting chamber – not a bad bit of engineering when you weigh just as much as a sigh.

The birds begin married life with an orderly establishment, but as time goes by, through the incubation period and the subsequent raising of the chicks, the tunnel and nest become a positive embarrassment, littered with fish bones and yucky bits and pieces of crustaceans. Not surprisingly, the adult birds head straight for a bath whenever they emerge. As for the chicks, well, you know how kids are.

The malachite's true glory, like that of its close relatives, lies in its bright plumage. Legend has it that originally kingfishers were all dull grey birds. A kingfisher was the first bird that Noah released from the ark. (Yes, I know, I also thought it was a dove; that's the trouble with legends.) As the bird flew higher and higher in search of dry land, it gradually acquired the colours of the sky.

DUGONG

The sailors of old, or perhaps short-sighted old sailors, regularly confused dugongs and manatees with mermaids. It's understandable. In the days of sailing ships the crew were often at sea for months on end, and during all that time there was never a fair maid in sight. Even the wizened first mate picking at the remains of his rotten teeth with the tip of a rusty marlin spike probably started to look attractive. So when the ship dropped anchor and a dugong rose from the sea, coquettishly shaking its whiskers, there must indeed have been a stampede to the ship's rail amid a cacophony of wolf whistles.

On his first voyage to America, Christopher Columbus wrote in his journal that he had quite distinctly seen three mermaids. He was off the coast of Haiti at the time, and to be fair he did also note, with more than a hint of disappointment, that he didn't think they were particularly beautiful, having rather masculine features.

Salty yarns aside, a much more likely outcome of such encounters is that the sailors would have done their level best to capture the dugong and haul it aboard, not to wine and dine it and shower it with roses but to slaughter the inoffensive beast for its oil and delicious meat. The dugongs of the East African coast have been hunted virtually to extinction, as has the African manatee, its close relation on the West Coast of Africa. Although they are both now legally protected, gills nets and illegal hunting still take their toll on the remaining small populations. The last dugong bastion is Australia's vast coast, which is home to about 80,000 of these mammals.

Dugongs are air-breathing and live in the warm coastal waters of the Indian Ocean, including the Red Sea and the Persian Gulf, and along the western edges of the Pacific, while their cousins the manatees hug the Atlantic shores of the Americas and West Africa.

The name dugong is derived from a Malaysian word meaning 'lady of the sea', perhaps intended to encapsulate their demure and gentle nature rather than any real or imagined feminine charms. A more literal translation, however, is 'lady in an outdoor bath', which does have a faintly voyeuristic ring to it.

The dugong is thankfully unaware of its role in the fantasies of sex-starved mariners. It lives a placid life, grazing on sea grass meadows in the coastal shallows, and has little in the way of natural enemies. Although capable of bursts of speed up to about 25 knots, the dugong's rotund shape is its principal defence, particularly against sharks; it simply turns its ample back on them, a bit like a society matron freezing out an undesirable at a village fête. The young do occasionally fall prey to sharks or saltwater crocodiles but these days are probably more likely to meet their end in a gill net or a collision with a motorboat.

Dugongs are social mammals and usually live in family groups of 3–10 individuals, although periodic large gatherings of up to 500 do occur where the population allows. The last such gathering off the coast of East Africa was observed in the 1960s, and such a sight is highly unlikely to be seen there again. Fewer than 200 now remain in Mozambique's Bazaruto Archipelago, and no reinforcements are on the way. They are semi-nomadic but, by and large, stay in the same general area their whole lives, moving slowly up and down the coast, drifting in and out with the tides to where they hope the grass is greener still.

Their long-term survival prospects are not enhanced by the fact that they are excruciatingly slow breeders, to some extent regulating reproduction according to the availability of sea grass, which is itself vulnerable to coastal pollution and trawling. A female dugong only gives birth to a single chubby baby every 5–7 years, after a 14-month gestation. At least eight years and more will pass before the newborn eventually reaches sexual maturity, longer than is typical of most other mammals. On the upside, if they can avoid catastrophic motorboat encounters and other artificial perils, dugongs can look forward to a long and hopefully uneventful life, a lucky few grazing through into their late sixties.

Despite the fact that even at a distance they are unlikely to be confused with Marilyn Munroe, dugongs seem to have captured the romantic imagination of more than just frustrated western mariners. In India their meat is believed to be an aphrodisiac, while in parts of Thailand people are convinced that dugong tears make a powerful love potion. Given the perilous future we've made for them, if dugongs ever cry, they most likely shed bitter tears of anguish.

BOOMSLANG

E ver since the apple tree incident in the Garden of Eden, snakes have been taking the rap for humanity's misfortunes. The boomslang is no exception, being particularly arboreal and seductively handsome.

If that's not enough, the snake is supposed to make a habit of dropping from trees onto rural pedestrians with the express purpose of biting them, a task it fails to perform with unerring consistency. It may, of course, be that boomslangs don't want to put themselves in harm's way by attacking a large inedible biped, a point that we tend to overlook in our stick-waving moods of righteous indignation. That said, in Africa there are lots of trees and lots of pedestrians and from time to time accidents do happen. Even in these rare instances, the snake is far more likely to mumble an apology and slither on its way than to bite.

The number of recorded fatalities notched up against the boomslang in the past 50 years would barely reach double figures, and most of the victims were professional snake handlers.

While Africans have always known that the boomslang is highly venomous, western herpetologists largely pooh-poohed this opinion until one of their number, Karl Schmidt, was bitten in 1957 by a juvenile he was casually and confidently handling. To his enduring credit Mr Schmidt carefully recorded what subsequently happened to him, a consummate professional to the very, fatal end. He had clearly never read Agatha Christie's 1935 novel, *Death in the Clouds*. It was the butler that did it, in the library, with a boomslang.

The boomslang is a member of the poisonous but otherwise happy family of Columbridae, but it is the only member that has the teeth and the chemical cocktail capable of delivering a bite fatal to humans. Its venom is primarily a slow-acting hemotoxin that switches off the body's blood-clotting system and causes internal haemorrhaging, including in the brain. Symptoms are slow to appear, so that someone who has been bitten may start to relax, think it's no big deal and not pop along to the doctor. This is a serious mistake. Without antivenin, the only cure is a total blood transfusion and, if left for two or three days, even that may come too late.

Another misconception, arising from the snake's petite features, has led some to believe that it is physically incapable of opening its mouth wide enough to bite anything bigger than a toe or finger. In fact, it can open its jaws up to 170 degrees, which is more than enough to bring the back fangs into action on an arm or a leg.

But enough of the scary stuff; the boomslang is a shy and retiring snake, certainly worthy of caution and respect but not to be feared. It is notoriously difficult to see, let alone catch, preferring to glide away through the branches rather than confront its tormentor. While boomslangs may come to the ground in pursuit of prey, they are arboreal snakes and will always return to a tree to enjoy their meal.

Newborn boomslangs are totally harmless to humans. They appear to have wriggled straight out of a Disney cartoon – grey with blue speckles and gigantic eyes that take up virtually the whole of their tiny heads. They start at about 20 centimetres in length out of the egg and seldom grow to an adult length of more than 170 centimetres. Adult coloration varies considerably, and they are among the few snakes in which the colour of male and female differs. Females are usually brown, while, confusingly, males can be green, black, grey or yellow; even the occasional pink one has been observed.

The adult snake's large eyes remain its most distinctive identifying feature. Unlike other species, boomslangs are thought to have binocular vision and are able to see their prey even when it is stationary. The slow and super-cautious progress of the chameleon, a favourite prey species, is consequently not much of a defence.

Unlike us, weaver birds have genuine cause to bear a grudge against the boomslang. It is very partial to their eggs, their chicks and, given the opportunity, the birds themselves. To add insult to injury, in the cold snaps of winter boomslangs are also inclined to commandeer a cosy nest in which to hibernate – a very literal case of being eaten out of house and home.

GUINEAFOWL

T he Lugbara people, who live in Uganda, make good use of guineafowls in their cooking pots and also in their many proverbs. Excessive pride made the guineafowl's head go bald, they say, meaning that presumption inevitably leads to humiliation. Oddly enough, another Lugbara proverb ascribes the bird's baldness to its being overly shy, proving that for every good proverb there is often another one to cancel it out.

In England's green and pleasant land the chatter of guineafowl presages sunshine and good luck, while in the pragmatic USA, free-range chicken farmers like to have them around, because they are better at spotting incoming eagles than the easily distracted domestic hen. Wherever they are, guineafowl make excellent sentries, setting up a cackling racket whenever they spot any kind of trespasser, airborne or otherwise, and even when they don't. Given the bird's propensity to let rip for their own social reasons, one has to make allowance for a lot of false alarms.

The birds were first domesticated in the lands around the Gulf of Guinea, and so choosing a name was a no-brainer. That said, under various local names they have been providing a reliable source of wild meat and eggs throughout Africa since time immemorial. They feature prominently in African art and are proudly, if rather repetitively, displayed on modern souvenirs from Africa, especially such mundane items as dishcloths, tea trays, place mats, oven gloves, salt and pepper pots, serving spoons, aprons, serviettes, tee shirts ... you get the picture.

South Africa is home to two species: the helmeted or crowned guineafowl and the crested. The former is traditionally an inhabitant of thorny scrub and savanna but is now seen all over the place, equally at ease in farmlands and in the leafy suburbs of cities throughout the country, wherever there is a reliable water supply. By contrast, the crested guineafowl is coyly confined in South Africa to the northern half of KwaZulu-Natal and northern Limpopo, where it spends most of its time in riverine bush and secondary forest and is far more shy and retiring than its peripatetic cousin.

Quite why helmeted guineafowl have been so successful in adapting to suburban living is something of a mystery. They have an unnerving propensity for running away from a speeding motor car only to abruptly change their minds and run straight back in front of it. Given the current standard of driving, that alone should have put them on the road to extinction. But the probable explanation lies in the total absence of jackals, pythons, large raptors and all the other predators that enjoy a plump guineafowl every bit as much as the Lugbaras.

The main visual difference between the two species is suggested by their names. The crested has a thick bunch of curly feathers on the top of its head, while the helmeted sports a bony crown that varies slightly in shape in different regions of South Africa. There are no obvious differences between the sexes of either species, and, by and large, they peck their way through the same menu. This consists of a wide variety of insects, snails, seeds, bulbs, worms and ticks. The helmeted sticks to the ground when feeding, while the crested is known to occasionally flap up into trees to feed on fruit.

Both species form large, noisy flocks, sometimes numbering in the hundreds. They break up into smaller groups when the birds go to roost in trees at night, reassembling the next morning. During the breeding season (from October to February) they stick to small family groups until the chicks have grown.

They are essentially terrestrial birds and usually fly only to reach a roost or, as a last resort, to escape a predator if running very fast fails.

Neither species is a great nest builder, a simple scrape in the ground under a secluded bush or hedge sufficing. A clutch of 6–8 eggs

is usually laid and incubated for 23 days. The young birds can fly after only 14 days, which may be just as well for the suburban dwellers. Hatching time is a bonanza for domestic cats, particularly those who have grown mighty tired of a monotonous diet of tinned pilchards.

The Ancient Greeks used to obtain the birds from North Africa, and the scientific name for the helmeted guineafowl is *Numida melegaris*, deriving from Meleagar, a mythical Greek hero. According to legend, Meleagar killed his uncles in an argument and was, in turn, slain by his own mother. His sisters were so upset by these alarming goings-on – and no doubt making quite a racket about it – that the goddess Artemis decided to turn them all into guineafowl. The distinctive white spots on the birds' dark plumage represent their tears.

BARN OWL

Nailing a dead owl to the barn door was one popular and predictably useless method of warding off evil on the farm in medieval Europe. In our own more enlightened times the barn owl is encouraged to set up home in the barn, even to the extent of the farmer cutting a hole in the eaves to give easy access to the rafters.

The reason for this agrarian about-turn lies in the realization that barn owls consume vast quantities of rodents, particularly mice, which might otherwise get stuck into the seed stocks and adversely affect the farmer's bottom line. The owls' close nocturnal association with witches and warlocks is now politely overlooked, or more likely dismissed as the nonsense it always was.

In many African cultures, owls in general, and the common barn owl in particular, are viewed as harbingers of bad luck, ill health and death and are associated with the seamier side of the black arts. The Balozi people, who live in the Caprivi Strip, believe that owls induce disease merely by being in the neighbourhood, while the Shona of Zimbabwe traditionally regard them as witches' birds. In Afrikaans the barn owl is sometimes known as a *doodsvoël*, which translates as 'death bird'. This gloomy label arises from the belief that when the owl emits its eerie call from the roof of a house in which one of the inhabitants is already croaking, death is sure to follow.

The great big eyes and the thousand-yard stare contribute to the sense of unease that many folk feel in the presence of owls. Add a teacher's mortarboard to its head, which illustrators of children's books often seem compelled to do, and you really feel as though you've been summoned to the headmaster's office.

An owl never looks at you from the corner of its eye; it always swivels its head to confront you head-on, if it deigns to look at you at all. The reason isn't outrage or indignation but simply that it has to do that. Owls don't have swivelling eyeballs; instead they have eye barrels, elongated tubes held in place by bony structures in the skull called 'sclerotic rings'. To make up for it, they can swivel their head a full and disconcerting 270 degrees. They have binocular vision and are able to see objects in three dimensions and judge distances as we do, but let's be honest, it's a bit like comparing our cheap knock-offs with their top-of-the-range Celestron SkyMasters.

Despite their impressive optical equipment, barn owls, like their strictly nocturnal cousins, rely on their hearing more than their eyesight to locate prey. The ear openings on either side of the head are asymmetrical so that a sound from above or below reaches one ear a tiny fraction of a second after the other. They are able to do the complicated math instantly and, by moving their head from side to side and up and down, can pinpoint the target, betrayed by a squeak or a rustle in the leaves, with astonishing accuracy.

Barn owls are in the Tytonidae, a separate family from the other owls, on the basis of anatomical differences and their distinct facial characteristics. They look as though they're peering out of a nun's habit (hence their other Afrikaans name, *nonnetjie-uil* or 'nun bird'), rather than through the pair of professorial spectacles preferred by many other owls.

Two species of the family occur in southern Africa: the ubiquitous barn owl and the grass owl, which is limited to Africa south of the equator. Barn owls occur just about everywhere in Africa, except for the Sahara and the dense forests of the Democratic Republic of the Congo, and also occur throughout the rest of the world, with the exception of the extreme latitudes.

The grass owl has a very different lifestyle from its slightly smaller and more abundant close relative. It lives and nests in long grass in lightly wooded country, especially near streams and vleis. By contrast, the barn owl often makes use of various artificial structures where it can gain easy access to dark, sheltered corners, such as mine tunnels, church towers and the lofts of buildings. Deserted hamerkop nests and caves are also favoured nesting and roosting sites.

One other peculiarity is that the barn owl usually lays its eggs at relatively long intervals, so that in a given brood the eldest bird may already have its feathers and be agitating for the car keys by the time the last egg is laid. Other owls follow more normal egg-laying procedures, though it has been noted that the chicks in a grass owl's brood can also vary considerably in size.

The barn owl has a vocabulary that consists mainly of screams, snores and other creepy sounds. This repertoire, together with its nocturnal lifestyle, and the fact that it often spends the day in dark recesses where vampires and bogeymen routinely hang out, is the main reason that the bird features so prominently in Halloween superstitions and folklore.

According to old English tradition, concoctions made from owls' eggs are supposed to cure alcoholism, whooping cough and, predictably, improve eyesight. Strangely, or perhaps fortunately for the owl, no such remedies could claim to instil wisdom.

CROCODILE

'How doth the little crocodile...' begins a short poem in Lewis Carroll's *Alice in Wonderland* . The answer is that it doth fairly well, all things considered. It has been welcoming little fishes into its gently smiling jaws for well over 60 million years and still manages to cling tenaciously to the IUCNs Least Concern list.

Crocodiles are routinely portrayed in folklore and literature as cold-hearted, duplicitous scoundrels, including in Carroll's sardonic little verse. Budding naturalists in the Middle Ages were partly responsible for setting the tone in their bestiaries and encyclopaedias, punting the idea that crocodiles hypocritically weep in a blood-curdling display of phoney remorse while devouring their victims. Shakespeare and other Elizabethan dramatists regularly seized on this imagery when making a point about their own unsavoury villains. Nowadays the phrase 'shedding crocodile tears' is usually and understandably reserved for newspaper articles about politicians.

As far as the crocodile is concerned, it is simply eating lunch. If it could give a damn, it would probably be perplexed at the sanctimonious opprobrium heaped upon its broad and scaly back and might well ponder where the real hypocrisy lies. It does indeed cry, mainly to lubricate its eyes, and there is some evidence that the act of eating can occasionally induce an incidental flow of tears. But anyone who has tucked into a particularly hot and spicy crocodile curry will be familiar with that phenomenon – it has to do with heat and sinuses rather than emotion.

The crocodile's image as a stealthy mugger is not helped along by the fact that it is stealthy and it is a mugger, lying in deadly and watery wait for unsuspecting passers-by. Mugger is another name for the marsh crocodile, claimed by some to be a corruption of the

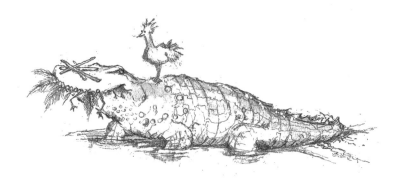

Hindi word *magar*, which means 'water monster'. This species lives in the Indian subcontinent and is closely related to the Nile crocodile. Muggers are infamous for balancing bundles of twigs on their snouts during the nest-building season in an attempt to lure waterbirds to within snapping range. They are not, by and large, held up as shining examples of moral rectitude, least of all in Rudyard Kipling's *Jungle Book* stories.

Though their numbers continue to dwindle, Nile crocodiles are still widely distributed in tropical African rivers and lakes. A few grow to awesome proportions, particularly in East Africa, reaching 5 or 6 metres from stem to stern and weighing more than a ton. South Africa is home to a few celebrity behemoths, but the majority of mature adult crocodiles in the wilds of southern Africa are less than 3 metres in length – still big enough to make a meal of large and unwary mammals, including people daft or unlucky enough to take a dip in their watery domain.

Crocodiles eat anything with meat on it, but their diet begins with modest fare. Hatchlings make do with tadpoles, frogs, insects and small fish, graduating to more substantial meals as they grow larger. Fish, especially catfish, form the main staple for most young crocodiles – no big surprises there, given that they share the same habitat. In their very early years they fall prey to a variety of other predators themselves, including fish eagles, snakes and adult crocodiles, which are not above snacking on their little nephews and nieces. Crocodiles only reach maturity at 12 and in ideal circumstances can live to be 100. Many years will therefore pass before a hatchling can hope to join the big bruisers assembled for events like the annual wildebeest migration across the Mara River in Tanzania.

Despite their heartless reputation, crocodiles are attentive mothers, at least in the limited sense of watching over their eggs and giving a helping hand with hatching. They need to be attentive, as many eggs are stolen by monitor lizards, baboons and other opportunists, with estimates putting this as high as 90 per cent in some areas. And while they are generally thought to be loners, crocodiles are in fact quite social in a snappy, mind-my-space sort of way, even cooperating once in a while to herd fish: they use the sweep of their tails in a slow-motion variant of the brainy dolphin's flamboyant and more complicated method.

In recent years, crocodiles and their American cousins, the alligators, have ventured into the luxury goods business. The downside of this radical departure is that they are the luxury goods. Their skins are widely used to make high-end handbags, shoes and other fashion accessories, while their meat finds its way onto a few select restaurant menus to satisfy the needs of curious, dry-eyed diners.

Crocodile farms are now big business. The only upside for the crocodile in having *Homo sapiens* as a midwife is that close to 80 per cent of the eggs hatch, and, barring diseases, most of the hatchlings survive. This has been particularly good news for alligators, thousands of which are released back into the wild each year in the Americas, where they had previously been hunted virtually to extinction. It is not a dignified state of affairs, but then again crocodilians are accustomed to surviving global ecological catastrophes, including the meteor that totalled the dinosaurs, and we are but the latest one.

MOLE-RAT

The annual convention of African mole-rats is an event that fortunately never happens. If it did, there would probably be a lot of infighting and turf disputes. Even worse, the proceedings would continually be disrupted by the startling appearance of a naked East African streaker.

Though the various species of African mole-rat share similar lifestyles, they are as different from each other as politicians and honest men. To add to the confusion, nobody seems to be completely sure just how many distinct species there actually are.

The naked mole-rat – and never did a name more succinctly describe its owner – lives in the sandy soils of East Africa, in communities modelled more on those of ants and termites than other mammals. A single breeding female and one or two sexually active males hold sway over a huge colony that can number up to 300. If you're not the queen or one of her studs, you're a worker, harvesting roots and tubers for the communal larder, or a soldier, charged with seeing off any unwanted visitors. The queen mole-rat keeps everyone's mind off sex and focused on the tasks at hand by her social behaviour, rather than by emitting a pheromone as some insects do.

In stark contrast, Cape dune mole-rats keep their clothes on, are a whole lot bigger and live solitary and cantankerous lifestyles. They have been causing havoc with transport and agriculture in the soft coastal sands of South Africa's Western Cape since the days of Jan van Riebeeck, who moaned about them in his journal. Using their clawed forefeet, they are mighty earthmovers and miners. A single individual can push up 500 kilograms of soil each month into many large sand mounds, excavating and maintaining an exclusive burrow system extending for 200–300 metres.

They are also fiercely territorial and drum on the wall of their private tunnel if they sense a neighbour getting too close, not unlike the solitary grump in the next-door apartment who wants you to turn the music down. During the breeding season the drumming changes pitch and volume, taking on an altogether more desperate tone that is even audible above ground. Connubial interludes are short and to the point, and the 2–3 pups that are born can't wait to get away from mom and each other after a mere couple of months.

Demurely placed between these super-social and antisocial opposites, common mole-rats try to lead a more-or-less normal family life, as much as that's possible when you need to spend so much of your time digging tunnels with your teeth. They live in colonies numbering up to 14 individuals, comprising a breeding pair and their offspring, though non-breeding house guests sometimes get to join the group. More widespread than any other African mole-rat, their subterranean kingdom extends across most of South Africa, Zimbabwe and the southern half of Mozambique.

Unlike moles, all mole-rats are vegetarian, feeding mainly on roots and tubers and, in a few cases, dragging down the whole plant, partly to eat and partly to use for nesting material. They can all happily munch their way through plants that are toxic to man and beast. Finding food is easier for some than for others, depending on where they live, a factor that helps to determine the social systems and domestic arrangements developed by different species.

Mole-rats spend almost their entire lives underground and are surprisingly well organized, excavating sleeping quarters, larders and toilet areas, apart from their vast array of foraging tunnels. They can beetle backwards almost as fast as they can forwards, which is pretty essential when the tunnel diameter isn't much wider than you are.

Despite this orderly approach and attention to personal hygiene, the atmosphere below ground gets pretty toxic, even worse than a locker room after a rugby match, particularly for the large mobs

73

of naked mole-rats. If you were miniaturized and popped down to visit them you would pass out in about 60 seconds and pass away a minute or two later.

The ability of mole-rats not simply to survive but to flourish in a low oxygen/high carbon dioxide environment has intrigued scientists, and particularly so in the case of naked mole-rats, because they live for a remarkably long time, up to 20 times as long as fresh-air rodents of comparable size. Some individuals of this species have been taking part in longevity studies in labs around the world for over 30 years and are still going strong. They don't get tumours, cancers or age in the same way as we do, staying fighting fit and feisty virtually all their lives. If it's any consolation, they are saggy-skinned and quite repulsive to start with, so much so that, ironically, Eduard Rüppell, the 19th-century naturalist who first described them, thought they were mutated or diseased examples of another species.

Foul air aside, life underground is safe and secure by and large, though mole-rats have to conduct regular repairs and maintenance to deal with rain and surface-impact damage. A predator may detect them from the surface and start digging, but mole-rats can run away through their tunnels and, as a last resort, have a pre-prepared escape tunnel to take them much deeper underground. No self-respecting jackal or hyena wants to spend the whole afternoon shovelling dirt to get down that far, as tasty a morsel as a mole-rat might be.

The main underground predator problem is snakes. Cobras and mole snakes, to name but two, take their fair share, but the real danger comes when mole-rats have to leave their tunnels and travel across the surface. This happens mainly when the young disperse, usually after the onset of rains, to find their own subterranean patch. If they're unlucky, a small army of potential predators stands ready to snap them up, including raptors and just about every other carnivore that happens to be in the right place at the right time. In suburban areas, swimming pools are a deep and present danger.

Although these little troglodytes don't generally impress with their looks, they play an important role in helping to aerate and drain the soil and in preventing the overpopulation of plant and animal species. If you believe the enthusiastic papers delivered at medical conventions from time to time, they may yet help solve some of our most pressing problems in cancer research and gerontology.

WHITE PELICAN

Pelicans were regarded as models of parental devotion and self-sacrifice by medieval religious thinkers. A popular motif in religious texts, carved in wood and stone or incorporated into the stained-glass windows of churches and cathedrals, showed the laudable bird pecking her own breast to supply her young with blood. A grislier version of the story, borrowed in part from Egyptian mythology, tells us that pelican chicks attack their mother, who totally loses it and retaliates by killing them. Filled with remorse and compassion, the parent bird then brings her delinquent brood back to life by wounding herself and showering them with her own blood. In this way the pelican became a powerful symbol of redemption from sin.

Quite where this daft and gory fantasy came from is anyone's guess. Perhaps some ancient birder, in the days long before binoculars were available, spotted a pelican on her nest dribbling fish guts and misinterpreted what he was seeing. Be that as it may, the behaviour of real pelicans bears little resemblance to that of their idealized ecclesiastical alter egos, which is not to say that they are bad parents, or at least no better or worse than most of their avian peers. In southern Africa, their main problem is finding a suitable nesting site at which to be any kind of parent.

White pelicans are big birds with exacting needs. An adult male can weigh as much as 15 kilograms and have a wingspan is excess of 3 metres, plus of course there's that whopping, one-of-a-kind beak. It takes a lot of protein to keep such a hefty assembly airworthy, and fish are harder and harder to find these days.

That's not their only problem. White pelicans nest in colonies on the ground in southern Africa and don't like to be disturbed. They are far from inconspicuous and hence need nesting sites out of reach of potential predators, typically jackals and hyenas. An uninhabited island in a freshwater lake is ideal, but those aren't easy to find either. One such fine estate in Namibia proved to be ephemeral, as the birds discovered to their cost. As summer rolled on, the waters gradually evaporated and eager predators watching from the shore were eventually able to wade over to the nesting site without even having to roll up their trousers.

Fortunately, pelicans are superb fliers, effortlessly covering more than 100 kilometres each day to and from freshwater fishing grounds, so an offshore island, like Dassen Island off the southwest coast of South Africa, presents a viable option. Here, the pelican colony shares the space with family-minded gannets, Cape cormorants and kelp gulls, among others. We all know that neighbours can be a problem, especially when they're raising noisy kids, but the pelicans have adopted a dark way of dealing with that: they eat the chicks, and even, on occasion, the other birds themselves.

Pelicans normally eat fish and prefer larger ones weighing half a kilogram and more. They often use a cooperative hunting method, seven or eight birds working in tandem and forming a semicircle in fairly shallow water to trap a shoal of fish. That famous elastic pouch is then put to work as a highly effective scoop. In ideal conditions, where fish are abundant, they can eat their fill within a relatively short time and spend the rest of the day preening and relaxing.

Times are tough in southern Africa, and the Dassen Island colony's behaviour is unusual by international standards, but far from unique. In 2006 a white pelican in London's Hyde Park casually grabbed and swallowed a live pigeon to the utter disbelief and consternation of a gaggle of genteel afternoon strollers. Elsewhere, from Australia to Mexico, pelicans of various species have been observed catching and eating seabirds and other unusual prey from time to time. In southern Africa, the alternative diet seems to have become routine rather than opportunistic, not just on Dassen

Island but also off Walvis Bay. The pelicans have even adapted their cooperative fish-hunting method when wading into cormorant and gannet colonies. Like it or not they seem to be doing well on this untraditional diet to the extent that their modest numbers have increased slightly in recent years.

When they're attending to their own intimate family matters, white pelicans usually lay two eggs, but more often than not only one chick makes it to maturity. The other dies, a victim of sibling rivalry and parental neglect. Notwithstanding the philosophical musings of medieval wishful thinkers, if the parent pelicans are upset by this routine natural tragedy, they keep it to themselves.

BABOON

Baboons usually make the news for all the wrong reasons, but once upon a long time ago they worked in law enforcement. Ancient Egyptian art depicts baboons helping cops in pleated skirts hunt down criminals and control unruly crowds. They were also popular as pets, and there is some evidence that they helped with the fig harvest.

In recent times, South African literature has been lightly peppered with examples of Chacma baboons behaving like model citizens. We can read about Jack, a captive male baboon who helped his crippled master with his railway signalman's duties near Uitenhage, even collecting a salary of sorts from the railway company. The self-impressed French explorer Le Vaillant tells quaint tales in his memoirs about his long-suffering baboon companion, many of which unintentionally put the baboon in a much better light than him. In *The Plains of Camdeboo*, author Eve Palmer tells us about conscientious baboon shepherds, while Eugène Marais, the biggest baboon fan by far, regales us with many quasi-metaphysical yarns about their enigmatic natures.

The occurrence of these cosy inter-species interludes has not, by and large, extended into the present day. Baboons living in close proximity to humans have long rap sheets that list an embarrassing array of offences: breaking and entering, larceny, malicious damage to property, lewd behaviour and even kidnapping. To be fair to the baboons, a good many charges are probably trumped up or at least exaggerated, particularly the one about kidnapping. While there have been isolated reports of baboons snatching human babies, notably by the inexhaustible Mr Marais, they have invariably given them back intact, rarely demanding much in the way of a ransom.

Baboons are not territorial, a difficult concept for human beings to grasp, saddled as many of us are with a whopping mortgage and an inordinate pride in our herbaceous borders. They basically hang out wherever there's a reliable food supply and somewhere safe to sleep at night, seeing no reason to move until they're pushed out. As our suburban mini-empires extend remorselessly into the wild lands, baboons have tended to become felons by default. Bungalows popping up in their home range, replete with well-stocked kitchens and delicious transplants from the local garden centre, must seem heaven-sent. It must be equally perplexing to find these treats fiercely defended by red-faced homeowners with yapping dogs.

Away from human populations, baboons continue to live their lives blissfully unaware of the need to conform to our social norms. Troops typically consist of about 50–60 individuals, though much larger groups are unexceptional. Baboons are big believers in the safety-in-numbers principle, a sensible precaution given that they

feature prominently in the diet of a variety of predators. Leopards, lions and spotted hyenas head the list, while jackals, pythons, eagles and other carnivorous opportunists bring up the rear, taking a steady toll on the young. Only 30 per cent, on average, make it to maturity.

Baboons lead complex social lives, intricate and varied enough to support or implode any number of complicated or airy-fairy theories. There's no doubt that adult males sort themselves into a dominance hierarchy, those with the biggest bulk and canines and the most testosterone predictably ending up at the top of the heap. Fights resulting in death or permanent, debilitating injuries are the exception; the opposition is more usually chased, stared or grimaced into submission. Troop females also form a hierarchy, though this, as one would expect of the ladies, is much more subtle and tends to fluctuate depending upon each individual's reproductive status.

To boggling human eyes, female baboons are the scandalous Lolitas of the bushveld. A female can come into oestrus at any time of the year, the bright red, swollen skin on her rump advertising her sexual readiness every bit as ostentatiously as a back-street prostitute waving a garish plastic handbag. She solicits intercourse by flashing the whites of her eyelids and presenting her rump to virtually any male who looks even faintly interested. Not all are, least of all the dominant male, who waits until he's sure she's ready to conceive. Everyone else then has to back off, so to speak.

In an attempt to squeeze a little romance from this rather sordid reproductive saga, researchers have pointed out that females sometimes consort with a single male for several days during oestrus, during which time they sleep and forage close to one another. The male in question may or may not end up as the father of her baby, but he does stand by her as a long-term friend and ally.

Despite the zillions of binoculars trained on the bush at any given moment, the birth of a baby baboon has rarely been witnessed. The female likes her privacy, and birthing usually takes place in a secluded spot at night.

There are very few critters cuter than an infant baboon. In a recent incident captured on camera, even a lioness who had just bloodily massacred a baby's mother turned sentimental, so it's little wonder that the whole troop takes an interest in bringing up junior, including, notably, dominant males, who seem particularly fond of playing with babies. But like everything else in the baboon world, things are usually not that simple. There are jealousies and squabbles, and it pays a mother to have built up strong social bonds with one or more male baboons. If a tetchy, high-ranking female takes an abusive interest in her baby, the mother can hopefully rely on his intervention.

A large troop of baboons has little to fear during the day as it forages in the savanna. Even lions will usually back off when confronted by a defensive group of large males. The night is another story, and baboons make sure they are safely bedded down in a large tree or on a precipitous rocky cliff well before sunset. If you creep up on them from below, they will likely give one final demonstration of their contempt for human social niceties by urinating on your head.

PORCUPINE

If you happened to be in a local restaurant and overheard the people at the next table talking about the Porcupettes, you might assume that your fellow diners were discussing a chubby female pop group. Instead they would in all likelihood be referring to the offspring of *Hystrix africaeaustralis*, the Cape porcupine, a rodent whose musical repertoire is confined to unmelodious snuffles, growls and quill-rattling. Despite this limitation, porcupines sometimes feature in the frequently opaque lyrics of popular music and have even bestowed their name on a progressive rock group that has incidentally enjoyed international fame and fortune in recent years.

Like most pop stars, porcupines are mainly nocturnal and enjoy considerable, though far less visible, success around the world. Vietnam is the only place where they're locally endangered, as people there eat too many of them.

Cape porcupines are members of the Old World porcupine family and live throughout Africa, with close relatives in southern Europe and Asia. More distantly related is the New World family, members of which live in North America and the northern areas of South America. The New World porcupines are differentiated by having their quills embedded separately, among other things, as opposed to the clusters sported by the Cape porcupine. American porcupines are also fond of climbing trees to feed on fruit, which seems a remarkably daring thing to do if you're covered in sharp spikes.

The name porcupine derives from the old French *porc espin*, which means 'pig with spines'. Being rodents, they are not remotely related to pigs, but their quills are without doubt their most prominent feature. The quills are sharp, can be up to 30 centimetres long and are more than a major nuisance if you're a predator trying to eat one of these creatures. Despite this, porcupines are preyed upon by a surprising number of other animals, including leopards, lions, rock pythons and even honey badgers. Some predators are more adept than others at coping with the prickly problems that inevitably arise, and all of them run the risk of being seriously incapacitated and ultimately killed by their meal.

Rock pythons seem particularly unlikely adversaries, but if they get the angles right they can happily squeeze the life out of a porcupine and then eat it headfirst, the backward-facing quills conveniently flattening in the right direction as the meal goes down. Being skewered by a few quills during the constricting process is normally not a fatal issue. The main problem comes if the python is disturbed once it has gone through all the effort of swallowing the porcupine and then tries to regurgitate its meal, as it instinctively does in an emergency. That inevitably ends in disaster. The snake also needs to choose a spot for its traditional after-dinner nap rather carefully – falling even a short distance off the rocks can be disastrous, what with a distended belly full of keratin needles.

The big cats usually fare reasonably well, so much so that porcupines form a small but significant percentage of the diet of lions and leopards in some areas. Care, as always, is the watchword. Quills deeply embedded in the mouth or paws can make eating and walking difficult or even impossible, all the more so if the wounds turn septic. More often than not, though, the cats get it right, and a face full of quills is not always the disaster it may appear to be. Unlike their New World cousins, the quills of Cape porcupines are not barbed and can fall out or be dislodged with due care and diligence.

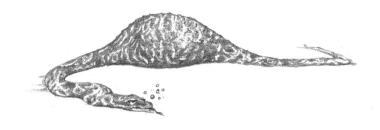

Porcupines defend themselves as best they can, but on the whole are shy and unaggressive creatures. They are sometimes solitary, but the normal family unit consists of a monogamous pair and their offspring. During the day they hide away in aardvark burrows, where such are available, and where not, in caves and rock crevices.

They're vegetarians, eating a wide variety of plant material including bulbs, fruit, seeds, roots and bark. They can be a pest as crop raiders in some areas, notably in Kenya where subsistence farmers have responded by adding them as a delicacy to the village menu. They also gnaw bones, crave salt and are occasionally attracted to campsite toilets by the smell of urea, probably something to bear in mind during your next hurried nocturnal visit to a long drop in the bush.

Porcupines don't feature prominently on the usual lunatic lists of animal-part aphrodisiacs, unlike the poor rhino with its low libido. This is fortunate but strange, as the one big thing a porcupine can look forward to in life is regular sex. The happy pair indulges in sexual behaviour every day, initiated by the female as a form of social bonding and to maintain her cycle. Subordinate females may get in on the action now and again but do not conceive.

Despite this daily activity, the breeding couple usually produces only one litter each year, comprising between one and three offspring. More often than not the result is a single, no doubt charming but decidedly uncuddly, porcupette.

EGYPTIAN GOOSE

The Great Honker was another name for the Egyptian creator god Gengen Wer who took the form of a goose and – apparently without undue stress or strain – laid the golden egg from which the sun hatched. With such impressive credentials, the Egyptian goose was inevitably regarded as sacred in Ancient Egypt, though sanctity didn't exclude these birds from having to contribute to a roast lunch. They were kept as domestic poultry by the Egyptians, as they were by both the Romans and Greeks, and featured prominently in their art.

In our own times of remorseless lists and reclassifications we are told that the Egyptian goose is not a true goose at all but more akin to a shelduck, though this does not appear to have affected its social status or lifestyle in any way. It still flies in the best circles and spends a good deal of time on the golf course and is consequently very widespread in South Africa, occurring wherever there are dams, lakes, rivers and country clubs. Unlike most golfers, its diet consists primarily of grass and grain with the odd worm or beetle thrown in.

As far back as the 17th century, Egyptian geese were imported to grace the ornamental lakes and ponds of some of the finest country estates in England, mainly in East Anglia. Small populations have lived there ever since. But hobnobbing with the landed gentry in a far-off land has not been without its problems. The immigrant geese kept their biological clock firmly set to African time and, in consequence, have continued to hatch their chicks in January. Their snooty avian neighbours probably look on in disbelief, given that every swan who's any swan knows this is precisely when nature dials the thermostat down to below zero, and foxes are at their most desperate.

In recent years life has started to change for the better, or for the worse, depending on your point of view. Thanks to global warming, January in Northern Europe is now increasingly survivable for Egyptian goose chicks, and the result has been a population explosion. The species is no longer confined to the gated splendour of English ancestral mansions and has joined the common waterfowl on village ponds in some other parts of Britain. In the 1960s some Egyptian geese made it over the English Channel to settle in the Netherlands, where conditions are much more to their liking, so much so that the breeding population now exceeds that of the UK.

Back home in Africa things haven't been going at all badly either. Large, loud and in your face if you dare to come too close, they are the most commonly encountered waterfowl in South Africa. In some areas, such as the wheat fields of the Western Cape, they have become numerous enough to be regarded as a pest. The birds are usually seen in pairs, but when there is an abundance of food, they often congregate in large numbers, the unruly crowd stomping on as many young shoots as they consume.

Egyptian geese are quarrelsome and bad-tempered by nature and particularly pugnacious in the breeding season. The male bird hisses, and the female honks, which is the one sure way to tell them apart. They are highly intolerant of other birds, including others of their own kind, and think nothing of smashing the eggs of an interloper who has the temerity to try to start a family in their back yard.

On a more positive note, they make exceptionally good parents, bonding for life and defending their brood against all comers, airborne or terrestrial, traditional or high-tech. In a recent incident in the Netherlands, the last picture the nosy pilot of a radio-controlled spy quadcopter saw before his craft crashed to earth was the face of an extremely angry Egyptian goose.

Egyptian geese use a wide variety of nesting sites, often recycling the abandoned nests of other species. They might nest on the ground, in matted vegetation near the water's edge, in a tree hollow or on a cliff ledge. Once in a rare while they choose an artificial structure, such as a ledge at the top of a church tower. This poses no problem when the time comes for the chicks to leave home. The parents stand below and call to them until they've summoned up enough courage to take the leap of faith. Whether by accident or sensible design, the chicks have been known to use drainpipes for the great descent, popping out at the bottom like fluff from a straw, maybe a little stunned but otherwise none the worse for wear.

A pair of Egyptian geese usually produces a clutch of 5–8 eggs, which are incubated exclusively by the female for about four weeks while the male patrols nearby, beak at the ready, looking for trouble. Shortly before they hatch, the mother starts chatting to the eggs, and the chicks in their shells respond. Perhaps they are learning to recite a spell from the Egyptian Book of the Dead, one meant for gaining access to air and water during the passage through the underworld. It includes the words: 'I have guarded the egg of the Great Honker. It is sound, so I am sound. It lives, so I live'. And indeed they do, hopefully forever after.

ZEBRA

War and peace, work and play, rain and shine, day and night, the horse has plodded, cantered and galloped its way through most of recorded human history. Until the early part of the 20th century it was present at almost every momentous event that helped shape the world we live in. Bronze statues of noble steeds now stand proudly in public places in most of the world's major cities, inevitably carrying an important bronze somebody or other on their back.

While the horse was building this epic reputation, its close African cousin, the zebra, managed to keep its head down and hence avoided being drawn into bloody battles and interminable parades. There were the odd exceptions. The first zebra to reluctantly reach Europe probably arrived in about AD 240 from a port in North Africa aboard a galley destined for Ostia, the ancient port of Rome. At the end of this dangerous, and no doubt uncomfortable, journey, the zebra took part in a lavish extravaganza at the Coliseum. It was marvelled at and then killed, most probably in an inescapable confrontation with an imported lion.

The Romans came to know the zebra as *hippotigris*, which means 'tiger horse' in Latin. The name we use in all likelihood originated in Africa, possibly the Congo, and entered the English language via Portuguese or Spanish during the 1600s. English speakers then liberally applied the word to describe a whole host of other things with black-and-white stripes, from fish to pedestrian crossings.

Being familiar in form and yet strange in appearance, the paradoxical zebra has long been a source of wonder and fascination. Modern scientific theory, based on foetal evidence, maintains that it is a black animal with white stripes, though feel free to argue if you've wagered on the opposite being the case.

This does not, of course, explain why it has such bold and dramatic stripes in the first place, something that seems odd, because it lives in a habitat where all the other animals do their best to blend in. Answering this puzzling question has become something of a scientific parlour game, and it's now possible to pick from a range of hypotheses, none of them mutually exclusive and all of them far from conclusive.

Early theories proposed that the zebra's stripes are a type of camouflage, helping to conceal the animal in long grass or dazzle and confuse predators when a close-knit group is surprised out in the open. More recently, the stripes have been explained as a way of fooling flies or as a type of air-conditioning, the alternating black and white surfaces absorbing or radiating heat to generate a cooling flow of air around the zebra's body. It may even be that the patterns, each as subtly unique to the animal as a human fingerprint, help them recognize each other, though there is not much in the way of evidence to support that particular theory. If it is true, we are left with the conundrum of how the other uniformly coated quadrupeds tell each other apart.

In any event, zebras don't seem to have completely made up their minds as to whether they like stripes or not, and if they do, whether broad ones or thin ones are more fetching. The quagga, a variant of the plains or Burchell's zebra, appears to have been in the process of losing its stripes altogether, incongruously sporting a pair of dirty white pants when it was hunted to extinction. Heaven knows what that did to upset the air-conditioning system or the fly-fooling apparatus, but it plainly wasn't working well as camouflage.

Cape mountain zebras chose to go in the opposite sartorial direction and have the most complicated and striking stripes of all, particularly on the rump; in consequence, their hides were much favoured as ornamental rugs. Thus, in the mid-1960s they, too, came perilously close to extinction.

Despite their close kinship with horses, zebras have always been – and still are – justly compartmentalized in most people's minds with all the other wild and exotic fauna of Africa. However, during the 19th century a few serious attempts were made to domesticate them. This proved to be surprisingly easy, or at least no more difficult than breaking in a horse or a mule. Though not as fleet-footed as the horse, zebras have greater stamina and, at least in the African context, are far more resistant to disease. These attributes appealed in particular to the military, and a few zebras were pressed into service as draft animals and even as mounts for soldiers. More visibly, Sir George Grey, Governor of the Cape Colony in the 1850s, had four zebras trained to pull his carriage and even took them with him when he was posted to New Zealand.

In the end, it was probably the zebra's muscular neck, nervous disposition and vicious kick that saved it from an ignominious life of servitude. Alice Hayes, a well-known horsewoman in the 1890s, recording her ride on a mountain zebra, best sums it up: 'The most awkward kicker I ever rode. It was no use trying to rein him back; he had a neck like a bull. He was far too neck-strong to make a pleasant mount for a lady'. Well, that's a relief.

CHEETAH

Charlemagne kept a cheetah as a pet and so did Cleopatra, Genghis Khan and Akbar the Great. Akbar reportedly kept 9,000, which seems a bit over the top, even for a 16th-century oriental potentate. In Hollywood during the 1930s it wasn't that weird to see a starlet clattering down the street in her high heels with a cheetah on a lead; it isn't that unusual to see one today in the Gulf states, cruising by in the passenger seat of a Rolls Royce convertible, jewel-studded collar sparkling in the Arabian sun.

As a fashion accessory or a living, breathing symbol of machismo, the cheetah is hard to beat. Of all the big felines they are the only ones prepared to behave even remotely like that ultimate species sellout, the not-so-humble domestic cat. Getting cosy with the human race can have its advantages. There are an estimated 600 million cats curled up on the world's sofas versus about 9,000 wild cheetahs eking out a living in Africa. A mere 100 years ago there were 10 times as many.

Cheetahs have long been flirting with extinction and, according to a current genetic theory, only made it through to modern times by a whisker. That whisker apparently belonged to a single female, the only one left after some unknown catastrophe decimated the species long ago. Not that we should feel particularly smug, genetically speaking. A similar theory holds that the number of human beings once dropped so low that we'd have struggled to make up the numbers for a proper post office queue.

Studies in the Serengeti over the past 30 years have revealed that cheetahs still depend on a few females to hold the line against the devastating infant mortality rate. Try as they might, many mothers just aren't up to the task of protecting and feeding their brood, and many go through their entire lives without successfully raising a single cub. The few supermums are a caste apart, managing to kill daily and feed their brood in the face of relentless pressure from lions and hyenas. In a few rare instances, they have even been known to take over as foster mothers when a birth mother has been killed or simply given up and walked away.

Cheetahs are justly famous for winning the cup as the fastest mammals on earth, but it may yet prove to be a poisoned chalice. The problem with doing 0–96 kilometres per hour in three seconds is that it takes an enormous amount of energy. Not only that, but you have to trim down the bodywork and jettison any idea of carrying heavy weaponry. The result is that the cheetah is a lightweight compared with the other muscle-bound predators that share the same turf. According to people who somehow manage to count such grisly things, lions in the Serengeti kill 95 per cent of cheetah cubs. Even the usually obsequious brown hyena sometimes robs them of their kills.

Cheetahs employ different hunting strategies depending upon the terrain. Their traditional method is to lie in wait, making use of cover just like any other cat would, until a suitable target, typically one of the smaller antelope, comes within about 50 or 60 metres of it. It then streaks in for the kill, knocking the hind legs out from under its quarry. It may sound easy from the comfort of an armchair, but the antelope is usually no slouch off the mark either. If it can run like the clappers and zigzag three or four times, the cheetah repeatedly overshoots and is soon exhausted. Even when successful, the cat needs to lie down for three or four minutes to get its breath back before feeding, fervently hoping that the freeloaders don't immediately start arriving with their knives and forks.

Despite these hiccups and drawbacks, the cheetahs' system works well in an ideal habitat – well enough to have brought them through from the Pliocene. The problem, of course, is that such habitats are continually shrinking or disappearing altogether. In Asia, they've virtually gone, and the Asiatic cheetah is all but extinct, a handful of highly elusive and gaunt survivors picking their way over the rocky slopes of Iran.

Although relatively easy to train as cubs, cheetahs are neither designed nor inclined to become household pets, unlike their diminutive distant cousins. For their survival now, they are essentially dependent on the wildlife sanctuaries of East and southern Africa, and those, in turn, depend for their existence upon the wisdom and goodwill of a notoriously fickle biped.

GROUND-
HORNBILL

The ground-hornbill is regarded as a rain bird in many African cultures, and the consequences of killing one can be dire, not just for the assassin but for the whole community. Goat herder Isidoro Ocak'amani was banned from his village in northern Uganda for 40 years and forfeited his rights of inheritance for slaying one of the birds and thereby causing a prolonged drought that decimated the local economy.

A regional and paradoxical variant of such tribal lore holds that the most effective way to end a drought is to kill one of the birds, recite various incantations and spells and then throw its body into a pool of stagnant water in the local riverbed. The stench is enough to cause the heavens to open and flush away the rotting carcass.

Whether the ground-hornbill, dead or alive, actually has any mystical meteorological influence is impossible for science to determine, but it is perhaps curious to note that the dramatic decline in their numbers has coincided with the onset of climatic shifts in many parts of its present and former range.

Large and prehistoric, with a prodigious predatory bill, the ground-hornbill is a walking advertisement for the increasingly convincing theory that birds are the direct descendants of dinosaurs. It first appeared in the fossil record in the mid-Miocene, some 15 million years ago and, despite the vast passage of time, does not appear to have found it necessary to invest in any significant changes since.

Ground-hornbills are the only habitually terrestrial members of the extensive hornbill family, with the southern ground-hornbill, *Bucorvus leadbeateri*, being the most committed of its genus to a pedestrian lifestyle. Nevertheless, with a wingspan of up to 1.8 metres, ground-hornbills are accomplished, if reluctant, fliers and when airborne show their usually concealed white wing feathers to startling effect.

They greet the rising sun with a booming trumpet blast that varies in tone between the sexes. The red throat sac inflates slightly when there's an especially fine sunrise and they feel it important to get out a really good blast. This heraldic duty complete, they set about their daily routine, which consists of walking sedately through woodland or savanna in search of something to eat. They rarely travel alone, usually living in groups consisting of a dominant breeding pair and two or three helpers, although this number can extend up to 10 or 12 individuals of different sexes.

They spread out during their perambulations through the bush, foraging separately but keeping the other members of the party in view, calling to each other if they do get separated. The standard fare consists of insects, lizards, frogs, snails and small rodents, but every now and again they combine to tackle something larger, capturing and killing big snakes, tortoises and small mammals. They particularly favour burnt patches where ready-made and pre-cooked dinners are often available for the undiscerning consumer.

Ground-hornbills are cooperative breeders, with the younger generation undergoing what appears to be a type of apprenticeship, possibly to prepare them for their own parental responsibilities. They

nest in a hole in a tree, though given their large size they need to find a substantial one, usually at the base, and sometimes have to make do reluctantly with a crevice in the rocks. For the same reason they skip the usual arboreal hornbill routine of plastering over the nest entrance, sealing the female and her eggs inside and leaving only a sufficient slit to deliver food. This is probably a sensible omission given that the equivalent of half a dozen bags of cement would probably be required to complete the job.

The female lays two eggs and incubates them for about a month, while her partner punctiliously ensures she gets enough to eat, assisted to some degree by other group members. Unlike her walled-up smaller cousins, she occasionally leaves the nest to stretch her legs and raid the fridge, during which interludes her partner takes over on the nest.

Only one chick usually makes it to maturity, the other inevitably giving up in the contest for food. There is some evidence that the weaker sibling is occasionally killed and even eaten by the parent birds. The lucky survivor spends three months in the nest and is fed by both parents and members of the extended family for a further nine months, a long stretch in avian terms and an investment in time and resources that may explain the instances of infanticide.

The long-lived ground-hornbills are hailed as good investment brokers in African tradition, though this has nothing to do with their forward-looking parental activities. When tribes were on the move and settling new lands, it was considered sound policy to find out where the hornbills routinely spent their time. Such areas were deemed the best land to graze cattle, the established currency and indicator of wealth in many African cultures.

The ever-expanding portfolios of cows, their owners and associated communities do not presage a particularly rosy future for the birds themselves.

DUNG BEETLE

No insect rose to such high eminence in the ancient halls of Egyptian religion as *Scarabaeus sacer*, the sacred scarab. The Egyptians believed that a cosmic scarab, a type of dung beetle, rolled the golden orb of the sun across the sky towards the west during the day and then trundled it through the underworld at night, attending to any necessary repairs and maintenance along the way. When the sun popped up in the east each morning, it was consequently as good as new.

The connection between celestial mechanics and a small beetle rolling a pile of dung about is not so obvious to the modern mind. But before pooh-poohing the idea, it is as well to note that painstaking and excruciatingly precise research has revealed that there is indeed a connection of sorts. Dung beetles apparently manage to roll their ball in a straight line by orientating themselves relative to the sun by day and the Milky Way by night. They need to keep to the straight and narrow in order to make a fast getaway; rolling a dung ball around aimlessly is an open invitation to other beetles to try to steal it, and none of them want that to happen.

Where there's muck there's money, so to speak, and there are hundreds of different species of beetle that make an honest living harvesting dung, as well as a disreputable few who make a habit of stealing it from others. They all prefer it fresh, and the droppings of herbivores and omnivores are especially preferred, having the best mix of nutrients. Hyena droppings, which are hard, white and mainly composed of calcium, can be safely ignored. Elephants provide a colossal bonanza, and an especially large deposit quickly attracts hundreds and sometimes thousands of beetles within a matter of minutes.

Not all dung beetles go through the laborious business of making a ball. Some simply dine al fresco, while others, of the genus *Onitis*, burrow a tunnel into the earth below or very near the dung pile, excavating an ample chamber at the end of it. They then selectively choose the most appetising items from the steaming pile above with which to stock their larder, just as you would presumably do if a supermarket fell on your head.

The rollers, as they are colloquially known, are thought to have evolved their takeaway method to overcome the intense competition for space one tends to encounter around dung piles, at least if you're a beetle.

The size of the balls some beetles manage to make and then roll away has long amazed observers, and all sorts of bizarre comparisons are made in an attempt to equate the feat to human experience. Suffice it to say that if you ordered a hamburger 10 metres wide and then rolled it a kilometre down the street without the lettuce falling out you would not only get into the *Guinness Book of Records* but would also gain some modest insight into what the beetles are up against.

The Egyptians believed that scarab beetles were all male and that they produced offspring by getting intimate with a ball of dung, a bit like a phoenix rising from fire, only not as ostentatiously romantic. Fortunately for the beetles and, let's face it, for the sake of common decency, this is not the case. A female *Scarabaeus* follows the ball-trundling male and waits patiently while he excavates a hole big enough to accommodate the dung. Whether she gives advice such as 'surely that goes there' will probably never be determined. When he's finished getting everything just so, she enters the hole to join him for a nuptial feast that can last several days. It may sound a bit gloomy, sans candlelight and a bottle of bubbly, but it's as good a way as any to really get to know one other.

With the feasting over, either the male or the female makes another ball, which the female alone takes down below (and the male leaves). After fairly elaborate preparations she lays a single egg in a hole in the near-perfect sphere, smoothing it over so that her grub will be snug inside and have plenty to eat when it hatches. An added bonus is that the outer layer of the ball will dry out and harden, in effect encasing an egg within an egg. She then departs, filling in the tunnel as she leaves, and scampers off to do it all over again.

Dung beetles are much admired by stock farmers the world over for their incidental propensity to recycle nutrients and aerate the soil, thereby helping to create verdant pastures for cattle and sheep. They are held in particularly high esteem in Australia where beetles imported from South Africa and Europe in the 1980s, presumably as highly skilled immigrants, are credited with a huge reduction in the population of pestilential flies, which are otherwise attracted to dung. A concomitant reduction in the number of Australian stock farmers feeling the need to wear silly hats with corks dangling from their rims has also been recorded. Everyone with even a modicum of fashion sense can be eternally grateful to the beetle for that.

LEATHERBACK TURTLE

An African legend, which varies in the telling but serves to explain the origin of turtles, informs us that a tortoise fled into the sea to avoid an eagle's wrath.

In the story, a king offers his daughter's hand to the first of these two creatures to bring him salt from a distant sea. The race day is set for a month hence, but the tortoise uses the intervening time to plod surreptitiously to the coast, fetch salt and hide it away at the finish line. On the way there and back he persuades other tortoises to position themselves at strategic points along the route on the day of the race so as to be conspicuous to the eagle. Come the appointed day, the two competitors set off, and the eagle is astonished to find that every time he glances down he sees the tortoise apparently more than keeping pace on the ground below. You know who wins. When the deceit is finally discovered, the tortoise flees into the sea where it has been hiding ever since.

This story makes a great deal of sense, excepting of course that it is difficult to understand why the king didn't simply marry his daughter to Prince Charming, like every other monarch in fairy tales.

Sea turtles have almost as many folk tales swirling around them as there are eddies in the ocean. Another popular theme is the mysterious island, replete with sand and palm trees, on which the Ancient Greeks bestowed the name Aspidochelone. Sea-weary mariners who came across this island invariably set up their barbecues only to find – just as the steaks were about ready – that it sank beneath them and was in fact a gigantic turtle.

Chelonia is now the name for the order of reptiles that includes all turtles, tortoises and terrapins, and the biggest of them all is the leatherback turtle. Although not island-sized, unless you're a shrimp, leatherbacks can sometimes reach a carapace length of 1.8 metres and tip the scales at 680 kilograms. They are further distinguished from other turtles by having a leathery, ridged carapace, as opposed to the hard shells sported by other, smaller species.

Leatherbacks cruise the world's seven seas with consummate ease and do not confine themselves to equatorial waters, ranging as far north as Norway, and southwards beyond the tip of Africa. Their large size and stored fats are assumed to provide a degree of insulation, and they are able to maintain a body temperature higher than the water around them, at least to some extent. This explains why they can function and venture into cold seas, whereas other sea turtles dip a flipper and quickly turn back.

Little was known about the leatherback's movements at sea until the advent of satellite tracking, but even now the trace of their journeys on the world's vast oceans is mostly a blank, like The Bellman's map in Lewis Carroll's *The Hunting of the Snark*. Tagging has at least revealed the remarkable voyages they're capable of, with one individual swimming 6,000 kilometres in under 10 months, from the north of South America to Ghana in West Africa, an average of 20 kilometres a day, not counting unknown detours.

Leatherbacks apparently know where they're going and where they've been, but what we don't know for certain is how they navigate. The open ocean is a featureless place, and any useful signage on the sea floor is far below and out of reach. Their above-water eyesight is poor, so it is unlikely that the stars in the heavens provide any points of reference, and scents in the restless sea are by the nature of things chaotic and ephemeral. The current thinking is that they navigate using the earth's magnetic field, like some species of birds are believed to do on an overcast day, probably fine-tuning by using other cues as they near their destination.

In the 1970s it was thought that the total number of leatherbacks was dwindling to the point of extinction, but other breeding sites have since been discovered, and some cheerful estimates put the global population as high as 100,000. This may seem a lot but isn't, given the size of the globe and the amount of garbage we dump in the seas every year. Despite their bulk, the leatherbacks eat mainly jellyfish, and our annual contribution to the fauna of the ocean includes tens of millions of plastic bags, which float on or just below the surface and look just like them. If you came back from the shops, tipped your groceries into the bin and instead ate the plastic bag, you'd soon get an idea of the problem this poses.

Male leatherbacks spend their long lives entirely at sea, but individual females come furtively ashore every few years, usually under cover of darkness, to lay their eggs in the sand. One favoured site is on South Africa's Maputaland coast where an estimated 500 female leatherbacks emerge from the pounding surf annually and drag themselves laboriously up the beach. Once she's laid her eggs, the turtle transcribes a mystic circle in the sand around her nest, just as the hatchlings will do when they emerge.

Life outside the egg must seem nasty, brutish and short for newly hatched turtles. Everything with a beak, teeth or claws is out to get them, on the beach and in the sea. About 1 per cent reach maturity, and only then does nature finally let up and bestow a measure of invulnerability – except of course, from humans.

Although they are protected in most countries, leatherbacks and other turtles are still hunted, particularly along the shores of the Indian Ocean. In Madagascar, poachers believe that they court misfortune if they kill one, but they do it anyway. To propitiate the turtle's spirit they cut off the head and impale it on a stick to face the sea, a home so close but forever out of reach.

BAT

Listing the different types of bat is a bit like the recitation of shrimp recipes in the movie *Forest Gump*. There's the banana bat, the butterfly bat, the fruit bat, the hairy bat, the horseshoe bat, the house bat, the leaf-nosed bat, the long-fingered bat, the slit-faced bat, the woolly bat, and that's more than enough for now. Altogether, there are over 50 species and subspecies of bat hanging out or flapping about in the night skies of southern Africa alone, and the count keeps changing. In the world at large, there are probably well over 1,000, perhaps a quarter of all mammal species.

Science has cajoled bats into two main groups: fruit-eaters, which have large eyes, two claws on each wing and a dog-shaped muzzle; and insectivores, which are generally smaller in size, have smaller eyes, big ears and a single claw on each wing. The insectivores all use echolocation to find their prey, whereas the fruit-eaters, with one exception, use their eyes and noses. All are nocturnal, and many of them roost during the day in the kinds of places and spaces that give us the creeps.

The good news is that none of them has ever heard of Dracula, let alone Gotham City. Despite this forgivable ignorance of popular Western culture, bats have had a bad rap for centuries. Only in recent years has the mood shifted to align more with that of the 'inscrutable Orient', where bats, including the flying fox, have always been associated with health, wealth and happiness, particularly in China.

Long before Bram Stoker penned *Dracula*, a babble of fabulous nonsense was believed about bats in medieval Europe. Because they looked vaguely like flying rats, they were assumed to carry disease, but mostly they were associated with witches, warlocks and taking tea with the devil and his demons. Poor old Lady

Jacaume of Bayonne in France was burned at the stake in 1332 on incontrovertible evidence that bats had been seen flying about her house and garden. If you're a myopic, sadistic pedant, you don't need any more proof than that.

Stoker simply needed to tap into a rich vein, so to speak, helped along by a newspaper article he'd read that described how a vampire bat had drained the blood from a child. It would be no mean feat for *Desmodus rotundus,* the common vampire bat, to do that. It weighs only 57 grams. It must have blown up like a rubber balloon and exploded, though the newspaper article in question makes no reference to such a gory postlude.

We need bats more than they need us. According to one estimate, seeds dropped by bats account for most forest regeneration on cleared lands in the Old World tropics. At least 300 plant species are known to be dependent on fruit bats for pollination and seed dispersal, including the fabled baobab tree. Without the sterling services of Wahlberg's epauletted fruit bat, baobabs would likely have become extinct.

If you really want to be impressed, get bats started on mosquitoes and other pestilential insects. South Africa's largest colony comprises the 299,999 bats that live in De Hoop Guano Cave near Bredasdrop in the Western Cape. They are credited with tucking away about 100 tons of insects every year, including many crop pests.

Over in the USA, Mexican free-tailed bats thunder out of large caves in central Texas each night, including the Bracken Caves, which host some 20 million, and chomp their way through about 1,000 tons of insects each and every night. They do things big in Texas. Included in the list of fatalities are millions of corn earworm moths, high up on the USA's Most Not-Wanted list of crop pests.

The lodging householders occasionally provide in return seems miserly in comparison, especially since bats don't spill coffee on the sofa, hog the bathroom or argue about which channel to watch on TV. Bats use a wide variety of natural nesting sites, but all those empty spaces up in the rafters where the geyser quietly runs up whopping bills are pretty much ideal, at least for some species. The vulnerable large-eared free-tailed bat, *Otomops martiensseni*, is confined in South Africa exclusively to roosts in the high-pitched roofs of a few double-storey houses in Durban. It needs a good address and a free drop to get airborne, so not every roof will do. These bats don't push their luck as lodgers, forming small colonies of up to a dozen individuals at most, usually females and a single male.

By way of contrast, the super cute banana bat, *Pipistrellus nanus*, though it lives in similarly small groups of fewer than 10 individuals, weighs no more than 4 grams and attains a length of just 80 millimetres at most. Banana bats routinely tuck themselves into the rolled-up terminal leaves of banana plants during the day and pay the rent by emerging at night to feed exclusively on insects.

There isn't much room in a bat's body for the digestive tract, so its diet is restricted to foods that are highly nutritious and easily digestible, be it fruit, nectar or bugs. Virtually all bats are fast feeders and big snoozers, seldom if ever seeing a sunset or a sunrise and dashing about in the dark for only four or five hours a night. They spend the rest of the time, an average of 19 hours a day, roosting under the covers. All animals are vulnerable when they sleep, and sleeping or snoozing as much as they do helps explain why bats seek out the darkest and most inaccessible places to spend the bulk of their largely somnolent lives.

One result is that even in our nosy world of scientific prodding and poking, the lives of most bats are yet little understood, leaving ample room for fear and superstition to flourish. Chiroptophobia (the fear of bats, not of chiropractors) is an especially popular neurosis, and the very idea of a bat getting entangled in our hair is a heartstopper for most of us. Chiropterologists confidently dismiss this as impossible, but it's not always wise to be dogmatic, particularly where bats are concerned. It happened to my mother, sitting in a cloud of mosquitoes on the veranda of a lodge in northern Uganda. The bat survived the entanglement and even provided an excuse, though it was scarcely needed, for a round of double brandies.

BUSHBABY

The tokoloshe is an African creature with nothing whatsoever to recommend it. In appearance, it resembles a little hairy man but is altogether more repulsive and malignant. Its nocturnal habitat is restricted to the borderlands between imagination and hysteria, and in this respect it can be assumed to be related to poltergeists and the other diminutive and imaginary nuisances of different cultures.

From time to time the rare capture and slaying of a tokoloshe is reported in African newspapers, but the corpse invariably and sadly turns out to belong to a galago or bushbaby, an inoffensive little primate whose resemblance to the mythical grotesque is restricted entirely to the coincidental fact that it is small, five-fingered, furry and seldom seen.

Bushbabies are by nature cautious, so much so that they haven't changed much in millions of years and chose to stay behind when the rest of us evolved into monkeys and apes. They even stayed put when Madagascar broke away from Africa and floated off into the Indian Ocean, taking some of their bemused relatives with it. Once the panic had subsided, the Madagascan branch of the family had little option but to make the best of things and evolved into lemurs, which now fill many of the niches occupied by monkeys in Africa and other parts of the world.

When you're cute, small, edible and not very fast it's probably best to stick to the trees, as indeed they do. The lesser bushbaby, *Galago moholi*, is the smaller of the two species that live in southern Africa, typically only weighing about 150 grams – snack size for a raptor, and a packet of peanuts for anyone else. The greater bushbaby, *Otolemur crassicaudatus*, is a whole lot bigger and sturdier, but still only the size of a small cat. Both have bushy tails that are a lot longer than their bodies and act as stabilizers when they leap between branches. When it comes to jumping, less is more. The greater bushbaby moves more sedately and conventionally than its smaller cousin, which hops rather than walks and can happily clear gaps of 3–4 metres.

Bushbabies have bulbous and enormous eyes that are fixed in their face like an owl's and sensitive enough to enable them to see by starlight, but they tend to stay put in the same tree on moonless nights, just in case. This has given rise to the accusation that they're afraid of the dark, which seems a bit rich coming from members of a quaking species that has populated the night with all manner of imaginary monsters. Most nights, dangers notwithstanding, they're out and about, even during thunderstorms, foraging within their home range, which varies in size depending on local conditions. It is never very extensive, as most of their modest dietary requirements are close at hand in the forest canopy.

Lesser bushbabies live mainly on gum exuded from holes in trees, the fresher the better, though they vary this chewy staple with the occasional insect snatched from the air or encountered minding its own business on a nearby branch. They can snatch an airborne moth or locust with lightning speed, closing their eyes and averting their face from its flapping wings like a human child being force-fed spinach. Their bigger cousins are also into chewing gum and crunching insects but add supplements in the form of fruit, nectar and seeds.

They routinely use the same arboreal pathways each night, mostly visiting a few familiar trees. They invariably forage alone, and individual territories are marked out in the time-honoured manner of urinating in the palm of their cupped hand and then dabbing the concoction on their feet and, when social convention demands it, on each other. The sticky mess has the added bonus of improving their grip. More conventionally, they also use scent glands to stake a claim at strategic points within their branchy domain.

Bushbabies are not especially social creatures, behaving more like a secret society than the gregarious members of a treetop country club. The basic family unit consists of a mother and her offspring of various ages who occupy a urinal home range. Adolescent males are booted out to make their way in the world, the more successful establishing their own territory that overlaps with those of two or three females whom they visit on rotation. The less successful often end up as something's lunch. The territories of dominant males rarely if ever overlap. Social arrangements up in the branches can get very complicated, and this probably explains why bushbabies are so emphatically committed to marking rights of way and boundaries.

They make a variety of vocalizations, depending on their moods and needs, but the distance call of the greater bushbaby is the most singular and arresting, sounding remarkably like a crying human baby. This sound alone is enough to have propelled the diminutive beasts into the realm of magic and superstition, evoking dim and misty recollections of our own beginnings.

CHAMELEON

A number of things differentiate lions and chameleons. Perhaps the most striking is that lions are a lot larger and don't usually try to catch their prey by sticking their tongues out. Nevertheless, the two creatures share a common name, at least in part. An Ancient Greek biologist must have thought the similarities were obvious, because the word chameleon derives from the Greek *chamai*, meaning 'on the ground', and *leon*, which means 'lion'.

Most chameleons are, in fact, mainly arboreal, though as usual there's always someone bucking the trend. The Namaqua chameleon spends most of its time on the ground on the arid and sparsely vegetated plains of Namibia and the sand dunes and bleaker regions of the southwestern parts of South Africa. Though similar in most respects to other chameleons, it can run very well, something it probably has to do quite often, given the lack of decent cover in its chosen habitat.

Nobody is quite sure how many species of chameleon live in southern Africa, although the current count is about 19. The great majority are dwarf chameleons, so called because they're smaller than the others, which are bigger and in the minority. If that nomenclature sounds a bit prejudiced and topsy-turvy, send your complaint in writing to the secretary of your local herpetological society. You may have to wait for a reply as he or she is probably out in the bush all day long trying to work out just how many different types of the little critters there actually are.

It should come as no surprise that new species and subspecies keep popping up, given their ability to blend in and remain practically invisible in trees and bushes by moving about at a bureaucratic pace. Their relative lack of mobility is one factor that is thought to have contributed to the evolution of so many distinct species, each confined to a specific habitat, with little if any overlaps. Some habitats are tiny. The very rare black-headed dwarf chameleon's perilous grip on existence was threatened when a business park was developed in the Cato Manor area of Durban in 2003, which goes to show just how bad things can be.

The most widespread and common species in southern Africa is the flap-neck chameleon, so called because it usually has a hand-me-down collar from a miniature triceratops. Its workaday outfit is emerald green and it's notably less knobbly than other species, many of which have prominent tubercles, crests or spiny ridges running down their backs. The flap-neck is the species most likely to be seen making a dangerous trip across the road in the Kruger National Park. Rather incongruously, its back-and-forth swaying makes it seem as though it's gearing up for a skip and a jump, which despite being physically impossible may well be what it has in mind given the nightmare position it's in.

Some chameleons are more kaleidoscopic than others, but they can all change colour to a greater or lesser extent. Changes are not only meant to enhance camouflage, which is good enough in most circumstances, but also to reflect their prevailing mood or to regulate body temperature. When two male Knysna dwarf chameleons meet each other on a branch, the dominant one becomes resplendent in radiant greens and blues, while the wimp tries to look less threatening than a baked potato. The imminent prospect of sex is another stimulus that sees both male and female chameleons rummaging through their wardrobes. The weather also plays a part. They are all diurnal and regulate their body temperature by positioning themselves to expose more or less of their bodies to the sun and, of course, by selecting the right outfit.

The ability to change colour is a neat trick, but chameleons aren't the only ones with such skills. Various undersea animals, including the octopus, are capable of more rapid and impressive displays. Perhaps the chameleon's most distinctive features are its extraordinary tongue, which it can shoot out like a party squeaker to a distance equivalent to its body length, and eyes that are capable of operating independently.

The optical control centre in a chameleon's brain must be a hectic place. Each beady eye rotates independently through 180 degrees, scanning the surroundings for potential meals and threats. When one side spots something, the head turns in that direction so that the other eye can join in, rather like swapping a telescope for a pair of range-finding binoculars. Cerebral pandemonium must break out if one eye spots a threat and the other a meal at exactly the same moment. Rather than take out the condiments and place mats, in such circumstances it's probably best to turn green and sway like a leaf, something chameleons do very well.

Although various mammals, including monkeys, are an ever-present threat, chameleons are mainly preyed upon by snakes and birds. Fiscal shrikes have the nasty habit of impaling small chameleons on thorns, a prospect marginally more ghastly than being caught napping and swallowed whole by an arboreal boomslang. With such unpleasant prospects in mind, and knowing that birds and snakes see the world differently, some chameleons seem able to tailor their camouflage specifically to counter threats from these principal predators.

In an increasingly frantic world and despite the dangers they constantly face, chameleons are determined not to be hurried and choose instead to live in a self-imposed oasis of calm. Living a generally languorous life is perhaps one thing they do, after all, have in common with lions.

SEAHORSE

A fantastical animal, part horse and part fish, was always a favourite motif in the mosaics of Roman public baths, popular in art and a talisman among the Picts who inhabited the British Isles. From the smug and condescending perspective of modern times it's easy to chuckle at the supposed naivety of the Ancients, with their weird monsters, and to marvel at the bizarre coincidence that a real fish with a head like a horse does indeed exist.

However, far from being confined to coral reefs and tropical waters, at least three species of seahorse live in the Mediterranean, including the short-snouted seahorse, *Hippocampus hippocampus*. This species also occurs, along with the spiny seahorse, in waters around the British Isles. It seems unlikely that the Romans or the Picts were unaware of them. Without TV and feature films to entertain them, they certainly indulged in bizarre flights of fancy, but they weren't ichthyological ignoramuses.

Forty species of seahorse are distributed around the world. Fantastic they undoubtedly are, with a horse's head, a chameleon's independently roving eyes, a kangaroo's pouch and a monkey's tail. They seem to be a product of nature's doodling pad. To top it off, they've got their gender roles the wrong way round and are the slowest swimmers in the sea, being unexceptionally overtaken by starfish, sea urchins and other achingly slow pedestrians of the deep. At first glance, it's amazing that they made it through the first week, let alone millions of years.

Part of the reason they survived is that very few things like to eat them. Instead of scales, they have bony bodies covered in skin, and some species have spikes and spines, so no doubt you, too, will be putting away the tomato sauce. They're also able to blend in, changing colour to match their surroundings, while some have

115

evolved all manner of accessories to resemble aquatic plants. One enterprising brown specimen purportedly changed into festive red to match the plastic Santa that aquarium staff had placed in its tank as part of their Christmas celebrations.

Seahorses don't have stomachs or teeth, so they live their lives like vacuum cleaners. To stay alive they need to suck prey constantly through their snout from the passing fog of plankton, fish fry, eggs and tiny crustaceans. They spend their days moored by their prehensile tails to seaweed or blades of sea grass, cautiously shifting between choice spots with a frantic boost from the tiny dorsal fin on their backs. The quaint process seems akin to a man using a teaspoon to paddle a canoe, but it's always worked for them.

What is more difficult to understand is exactly why male seahorses got lumbered with the kids, all 200 of them. Nature has a funny way of doing things, but somewhere along the evolutionary line it must have seemed a good idea. The female still produces the eggs, but she lays them in a pouch on the male's abdomen and then goes shopping. He has to do the rest, fertilizing the eggs and then putting up with the mayhem, until one fine day they all pop out, anything from a dozen to a small army of exact replicas, depending on the species. Sympathetic scientists have speculated that the reason for this strange arrangement isn't simply that the ladies have managed to pull a fast one. Producing eggs is an energy-intensive business, and if the male plays a bigger part in the reproductive process instead of goofing off on the golf course, the whole species is a winner.

During the breeding season the male is pregnant for most of the time. As soon as one lot of kids have collected their diplomas and floated off to make their way in the world, the female deposits another batch of eggs. Understandably, the male tends to stay put, nursing his big belly and maybe a headache, and the female keeps him sweet by visiting each morning just to show she cares. There is some evidence that seahorses are monogamous, which is perhaps not surprising given the scale of their mutual investment. Also, in small populations it's not always easy to find a mate, so if pops dozes off, loses his grip and floats away into the wide blue yonder, the female can have a problem.

Seahorses need an edge, now more than ever before. As adept and innovative as they are at reproducing, they're still in danger of being overwhelmed by our insatiable appetite for their corpses. Desiccated seahorses make good key rings and all manner of other curios, if you like that macabre kind of thing. Hundreds of thousands find their way into the trinket trade each year, but that's a drop in the ocean compared with the 20 million that end up ground into powder and sold in Asia as a cure for everything from broken bones to broken hearts. The surge in demand in China has coincided with that country's economic boom and rapid modernization, beginning in the 1980s. Paradoxically, powdered seahorse was once used in Western medicine, but the practice petered out at the onset of the Industrial Revolution.

Southern Africa is thought to be home to about five fragile species, the best known being the Knysna seahorse, *Hippocampus capensis*, which is further distinguished by being the only species in the world entirely restricted to a small estuarine habitat. The Knysna seahorse has its own set of problems. Unfortunately, the lagoon is slap bang in the middle of one of South Africa's most rapidly developing playgrounds, replete with motorboats, land reclamations and oops-it-wasn't-us streams of effluent. At the moment the seahorse population seems to be managing, but the grip of their tails on blades of sea grass has probably tightened to knuckle white.

MONITOR LIZARD

The earliest recorded instance of a monitor lizard being kept as a pet comes to us in the form of a story from the borderlands of India and Bangladesh.

Dawa, the founder of a clan of the Garo tribe, captured a baby water monitor and put it in a cage. On each of the days that followed, the lizard's concerned parents came to visit their imprisoned offspring. Astonished by their enormous size, Dawa grew increasingly worried they would take revenge. He finally released the young monitor, gave it a yellow coat and a set of earrings, and promised the parents that he would never capture one again. In return they promised not to harm him or his family. In a postscript, we learn that Dawa and the young monitor became firm friends and when the lizard grew up it often carried him across the river on its back.

Recent developments in Palm Beach County in the State of Florida do not seem set for such a happy outcome. *Varanus niloticus*, the Nile or water monitor, imported into Florida from Africa by dealers in exotic pets, have found their way out of cages and condos and into a habitat very much to their liking. Included on their New World grocery list are domestic cats, a sensitive food choice that has led to violent confrontations between the reptiles and gun-toting local law enforcement, not to mention creating angst among the bejewelled retirees of Palm Beach County.

Explaining why anyone would want a Nile monitor as a domestic pet is a conundrum best left to professionals. Like most species they're cute when they're small, but they grow up to be the biggest lizards that Africa has to offer. An adult has jaws like a steel trap, claws capable of slicing your arm to the bone and a muscular tail it can swing like a baseball bat.

Monitors are more closely related to snakes than to lizards and have the forked tongue and the venom to prove it, albeit in doses too small to be lethal to humans. But not to worry, they may also have a mouth full of salmonella, streptococcus and a host of other bacteria to make up for the deficiency. To top it off, they don't like people or anything else for that matter, including each other most of the time. Even their nuptials are fraught with dangers. If you want to kiss and cuddle a Nile monitor you had best be prepared for a medical emergency.

Monitors purportedly got their name because of a mix-up in translation between Arabic and German, but the general consensus is that they're named for their habit of watchfulness; they seem to continually monitor their surroundings for dangers and opportunities. The Ancient Egyptians would probably have concurred. They apparently tethered monitors to the banks of the Nile as a kind of crocodile early-warning system. If the lizard remained placid, it was safe to swim, but if it became agitated it was taken as a sign that a crocodile was lurking nearby. Dutch explorers thought they looked like iguanas and they hence became known as *leguan* in Afrikaans.

There are about 78 known species of monitor lizard in the world and by far and away the largest is the Komodo dragon, which lives on various islands in Indonesia and eats water buffalo. Let me quickly add that, big as it is, the Komodo doesn't swallow them whole. It dashes in and inflicts a bite that invariably causes an infection so virulent that the hapless buffalo keels over in a couple of days. The humongous lizard then feeds at its leisure.

Africa is home to two species, the water monitor and the rock monitor, *Varanus albigularis,* which is a little smaller than its closely related cousin. As their names suggest, they occupy different habitats. The water monitor lives in close proximity to rivers, swamps, lakes and pools, as well as along the seashore throughout Africa, while its cousin favours the bush, feeling particularly at home in rocky terrain. Both species are accomplished tree climbers and spend a good deal of time basking on branches. A water monitor often chooses a branch overhanging a riverbank so that it can drop straight into the water if it has to, or into a canoe being paddled quietly along underneath, as was reported in one alarming case.

Water monitors are solitary creatures, but they sometimes cooperate to steal eggs from a crocodile's riverbank nest. One lizard pulls reptilian faces at the croc and, when the offended monster indignantly lunges after it, the other darts in behind, digs like crazy and helps itself. They then purportedly swap roles. A type of plover, appropriately and colloquially known as a *dikkop* or thickhead, is known to lay its eggs on the ground close to a crocodile's nest, presumably in the hope that the brooding crocodile will be uninterested in the bird's modest clutch and scare off any possible predators simply by being there and looking ferocious. We can assume that the canny water monitors thus also get to enjoy an occasional side dish.

When it comes to laying their own eggs, water monitors take sensible precautions. They look for an active termite mound and, if one is available, break a hole in the wall and deposit their eggs

120

inside. For some reason, the termites don't attack the clutch and instead set about repairing the damage, thereby sealing up the eggs in a safe, humid and temperature-controlled environment.

The young can take up to a year to hatch. When they do, they make their way through the termite's air-conditioning ducts like burglars leaving a heist, probably snacking on termite guards along the way. There has been speculation that the mother returns to free the hatchlings, but this would presuppose an uncanny sense of timing, let alone a remarkable memory. Like her rock monitor cousin, who simply buries her eggs in a hole, she probably forgets all about them.

Monitor lizards play different roles in the folklore of disparate peoples, varying from benign to evil. In Borneo, if a monitor lizard comes between two warring tribes they call off the battle, and that can only be good. In parts of Pakistan it's best to keep your mouth firmly shut if you encounter a monitor; if it sees your teeth it can somehow steal your soul.

Some believe that monitors' flicking tongues gave rise to the idea of fire-breathing dragons, mythical creatures that themselves have enigmatic and contrary reputations. Although there are other credible candidates for that distinction, monitors do have an otherworldly look about them. The monitor was the first animal to come ashore 40 years after the devastating volcanic eruption of Krakatau, easing itself up out of the waves onto the primordial and sterile cinders. What drew it to such a wasteland, nobody knows. It can't possibly have mistaken it for Palm Beach.

GIRAFFE

If the giraffe didn't exist we probably couldn't invent it. The Ancient Greeks, who were always up for an intellectual challenge, nevertheless gave it a try. They had to rely on Egyptian travellers' tall tales, because they'd never laid eyes on a live one. The result was a cross between a camel and a leopard. Even in a daydream that sounds like a biological and mechanical impossibility, so they consigned their hybrid to the realm of myth.

The Egyptians knew better. Ramses II had one in his menagerie, a prize possession somehow transported down the Nile from the East African savanna. Giraffes are by nature nosy parkers, better adapted to seeing over the heads of the crowd than any other animal, so the pharaoh's delightful and unusual pet probably found the sights and sounds of Giza fascinating.

Giraffes were eventually introduced to Europe via circuses, zoos and private collections and, although always rare, settled into the ordinary European mind as bizarre but nevertheless real rather than imaginary creatures.

A problem arose when Charles Darwin returned from his trip on the *Beagle*, clutching copious notes and boxes of samples and then sat down and wrote *On the Origin of Species*. The book went through several editions and in the sixth one Darwin decided to tackle the giraffe. Not everyone had found his theory of evolution credible, and his opponents seized on the one-of-a-kind giraffe as a glaring example to argue that evolution was codswallop. Darwin maintained that the giraffe had evolved to feed from the tops of trees and wrote: 'By this process long-continued, which exactly corresponds with what I have called unconscious selection by man, combined no doubt in a most important manner with the inherited effects of the increased use of parts, it seems to me almost certain that an ordinary hoofed quadruped might be converted into a giraffe.' So began a verbose debate that still rages to this day.

The problem with giraffes is that they have no close living relatives and are so radically different from everything else. Even the fossil record hasn't turned up much in the way of clues. Evolutionists breathed a sigh of relief when the okapi, sporting a zebra's bum and a long neck, emerged from the Congo forest to astonish the world in 1901. The okapi was quickly bundled into the same family as the giraffe, but not everyone's convinced.

Giraffes, and for that matter okapis, don't always abide by the evolutionary rules laid out for having such an extraordinary neck. For a start, female giraffes are on average about a metre shorter than males. The young, of course, are even shorter, and either they're getting the short end of the stick, so to speak, or neck length doesn't matter as far as survival is concerned. It has also been pointed out that giraffes don't always, or even usually, eat from the tops of trees anyway. Females frequently eat with their necks almost horizontal. Only the big bulls routinely stretch up for the presumably delectable leaves at the tippy top and in the process lose sight of what's going on down below. This may partly explain why nearly twice as many male giraffes as females fall victim to lions.

With their compelling urge to have a unique perspective on what the neighbours are up to, giraffes seem to have done some kind of private deal with nature. Being on stilts has its downside, of course, not least when they want to drink. When that happens they need to lower their head through 4.5 or 5 metres and then whip it back up again every few seconds to check that there isn't anything sneaking up on them. That would be enough to make anyone dizzy, but giraffes cope with the problem by having a unique circulatory system. Their hearts beat 150 times a minute, and a complicated system of valves, overflows and elastic artery walls ensures enough blood stays in the brain to prevent them from seeing stars and keeling over.

Nature drew the line at providing parachutes, and a newborn giraffe consequently has to drop into the world with a bit of a bump. Like the young of most species, they're fortunately tougher than they look and in a matter of seconds work out that all those wobbly and bendy poles on what must be their bottom half are actually legs. They're up soon enough, already 1.8 metres tall and able to totter after mum as she moves off to check out what everyone else has been up to in her absence.

Young giraffes are weaned at about seven months and stay with their mothers for two or three years. The other adults do their own thing, drifting together and then moving apart in a constant shuffling of the groups within each local community. They don't seem to want to miss out on any gossip, but they also like their space and rarely bunch up in the manner of other ungulates.

Mature bulls are prone to wander on their own, though they seldom miss an opportunity to poke their nose into a passing female's business to check whether she's ready for a bit of slap and tickle. Young males are more likely to hang out together, indulging in occasional neck-wrestling matches to establish or maintain a dominance hierarchy, something that's usually more or less sorted out early on in the life of their given community.

Only when a large bull wanders in over the horizon do things get hectic. The local dominant bull and the interloper square up, standing side by side and use their heads to wallop each other's bellies and flanks with pendulum blows. Such choreographed battles are very seldom fatal, but the sound of each impact can be heard a good distance away, not infrequently attracting the attention of lions that then amble over with their own agenda. Lions are a perennial pain in the neck as far as giraffes are concerned, but a problem that comes with the territory.

While returning the stare of a giraffe, it's easy to imagine it'd be amused if it knew of the controversy that rages around the question of how and why giraffes got to be as they are. Despite their imposing height, they don't look down their noses, and their expression never seems arrogant or superior. Their soulful eyes and charming demeanour suggest instead a kind of benevolent curiosity, as befits one of the world's most curious creatures.

FLAMINGO

When considering the flamingo, it's difficult to decide whether nature was cracking a joke or showing off. How a bird that apparently shares its ancestry with the diminutive grebe could be persuaded to get up on stilts, turn its beak upside down and kit itself out for a gay parade is one of life's enduring puzzles. Flamingos are ungainly and yet elegant, garish and yet gorgeous; they can raise a laugh or reignite the smouldering souls of poets. It comes as no surprise that Lewis Carroll chose to employ them as croquet mallets in the illogically logical world of *Alice in Wonderland*.

There are six extant species of flamingo, and they are all, by and large, cut from the same colourful cloth and follow the same basic design. A seventh type, Featherstone's flamingo, is differentiated by the fact that it's made of plastic. It can be found on manicured lawns in suburban America, usually singly or in pairs but sometimes in flocks. Originally created in 1957 by Don Featherstone for the garden ornament company Union Products, the current population of indestructible pink plastic flamingos is estimated to run into millions. While reviled by many as the pinnacle of kitsch, the Smithsonian recognizes the enigma as an icon of American folk art, and in 2009 it was adopted, believe it or not, as the official plastic bird of the City of Madison in the State of Wisconsin.

Real flamingos are not endemic to the USA, least of all Wisconsin, and traditionally favour tropical and subtropical climes. The closest naturally occurring populations of American flamingos, *Phoenicopterus ruber*, are found on islands in the Caribbean. Three other New World species live further south, notably in Chile. The exotic and appealing vision of paradise that the birds conjure up in the jaded minds of commuting America probably explains the enduring appeal of Mr Featherstone's immobile replicas.

The world's most widespread living and breathing species is the greater flamingo, *Phoenicopterus roseus*, which occurs in isolated communities in many parts of Africa, southern Europe and southeast Asia. The most numerous is the lesser flamingo, *Phoeniconaias minor*, particularly famous for gathering in vast flocks, numbering in the tens of thousands, on the inhospitable soda lakes of East Africa's Great Rift Valley. Where they overlap, including in South Africa, the two species are sometimes found together, sharing the same habitat.

Both species are filter feeders but largely target different prey and so have no reason to get testy with each other. The lesser flamingo feeds mainly on plankton and algae, while the bigger bird tucks into small aquatic invertebrates, insects and tiny fish, but their method of feeding is essentially the same. They dip their bristle-lined topsy-turvy bill into the water and sweep it to and fro like a sieve. Their tongue acts like a piston to pump out the water, and the bird then swallows the mush. Baby flamingos are born with light grey plumage

and the pinks and reds of adult birds are derived mainly from the carotene and bacteria in their diet. Generally speaking, the pinker the flamingo the better it's fed and the happier it probably feels.

All flamingo species are gregarious, which is just as well, because nature has been remarkably stingy in providing habitats to meet their preferred feeding, breeding and security requirements. The ideal combination sometimes leads them to places that most other birds, animals and even most fish would regard as hell on earth. Soda lakes, like those in the Great Rift Valley, typically have few, if any, large fish to compete for the organisms the birds feed on. The catch is that such lakes often have no outlet, and if the inflow of fresh water drops, the salts remorselessly build up. At the best of times the birds have to visit nearby streams regularly to clean their plumage. In bad years the saline balance can get so out of kilter that it dooms the chicks. Salt gradually builds up on their legs, eventually forming heavy manacles that make walking difficult and the prospect of flying impossible.

Aside from such gloomy natural traps, things usually work out, and the birds are capable of staging some of the biggest and most flamboyant parties on the planet. Their en masse synchronized mating rituals can be hilarious to our eyes, though they'd probably be mortified to hear it. But they've got the moves, baby, easily outshining a heaving mass of self-conscious teenage disco dancers.

The point of these synchronized displays is to pair off and get everyone in the mood. Once the fun's over they get down to the serious business of nest building. The result is a mini-volcano made mainly of mud. The female lays a single egg in the caldera, and the parents take turns sitting on the nest. Both parents feed the chick for several weeks with crop milk manufactured by glands in their upper digestive tract; they are among the few birds to have evolved such an intimate method.

Flamingo chicks instinctively know that they're one of a crowd rather than one of a kind, congregating into small neighbourhood crèches within two weeks of hatching. Where there's a large population, these small crèches gradually coalesce into a super-group containing all the chicks in the colony. The purpose, of course, is to counter the threat from predators, but fish eagles, jackals and hyenas like to pop in now and again to point out the deficiencies.

A flamingo chick can potentially look forward to a remarkably long life, although there are no guarantees in the wild. A male greater flamingo that arrived in the Adelaide Zoo in Australia in 1933 finally died in 2014, at the ripe old age of 83. At the time, he was the oldest creature in the zoo, a martyr to arthritis. His sole companion over many years was an Andean flamingo that, at a sprightly 65, still soldiers on alone.

FISH EAGLE

E agles used to be regarded as messengers of the gods and still
are in some cultures, including in Africa. In South America, the
Aztec god Huitzilopochtli despatched an eagle to help with the site
plan for Tenochtitlan, their capital city. The bird sat on a cactus and
ate a snake, and that was apparently more than enough inspiration
for city engineers. On the other side of the Atlantic, Zeus sent an
eagle from Olympus to kidnap Ganymede, a Greek shepherd boy,
apparently because the lad was easy on the eye, and the god thought
he'd make a good drinks waiter, among other things.

Nowadays eagles have better ways to spend their time than
carrying notes and running errands for the gods, the import of
which are invariably ambiguous and at worst downright sinister.
The birds nevertheless continue to soar through the human
psyche as symbols of the mystic, military and majestic. They
have led Roman legions into battle and down through the ages
have been represented on innumerable flags and standards,
wings outstretched, grasping all manner of military symbols and
paraphernalia in their talons.

The African fish eagle features in the coat of arms of no fewer
than three African countries, two in the south and one in the north,
giving a rough idea of the bird's extensive distribution. Its image is
evoked in countless commercial contexts, peddling everything from
luxury tourist lodges to spare tyres. For many, the distinctive call of
the fish eagle is the sound that most evokes Africa, even beating out
a lion's roar, if only by a whisker.

Not bad for a kleptoparasite. Despite their regal status, African
fish eagles clearly don't feel constrained by the notion of noblesse
oblige and make a regular habit of robbing other fish-eating birds
of their catch. Among their nonplussed victims are pied kingfishers,

130

Goliath herons and saddle-billed storks. Their thieving proclivities don't end there. They have been known to steal prey from other raptors, including the odd snake from a martial eagle.

Fish eagles are also partial to the plump waterfowl that share their domain. Species that need to keep a particular lookout for an unwelcome, and often fatal, royal visit include coots, grebes and ducks, but the list of potential victims, avian and otherwise, is virtually endless. On the salt lakes of East Africa's Rift Valley, fish eagles often dine on flamingos, both chicks and adults, recalling the banquets of Imperial Rome where platters of flamingo tongues were a regular item on the emperor's table.

Day-to-day fare is more humdrum and plebeian. Depending on the locale, the bulk of a fish eagle's diet consists of fish, which it catches itself. As we can expect of a bird that Hollywood would struggle to invent, the eagle accomplishes this routine task with majestic aplomb. Descending from on high in a shallow dive, it seems to tear a slit in the still, golden surface of the water with its talons and effortlessly extract a silver and slippery prize. Well, that's what the script says. Sometimes it works, and at other times the bird grabs hold of a glutinous mullet or a catfish that has never heard of Weight Watchers. About 2 kilograms is the upper limit for an aerial lift; above that and the bird resorts to rushing the fish along the surface to the nearest bank. Even heavier and it has to struggle ignominiously to shore with its tubby catch using its wings as paddles. It doesn't always have a choice. It's sometimes stuck to its lunch, because its feet are lined with small barbs, whose function is to prevent prey from slipping away.

Although widespread in Africa, fish eagles are restricted by their basic needs to the vicinity of large lakes and dams, estuaries and the banks of perennial rivers. Immature birds are an exception. Rather like adventurous backpackers, they often pop up where they're least expected, perhaps choosing to see more of the world but more likely driven out by bossy adults. The greatest concentrations of breeding pairs occur in Botswana's Okavango Delta and in the Great Lakes region of East Africa. South Africa, with its relative dearth of large rivers and lakes, has a small population, estimated to number no more than 500 pairs.

Fish eagles are monogamous and highly territorial, usually establishing their throne at the top of a tall tree as near as possible to the water's edge. On the huge artificial lake of Kariba, between Zambia and Zimbabwe, they occasionally opt for a moat and build their nest on a dead tree standing in the water. A pair of birds may have two or more waterfront properties within their territory, which they use in rotation, but more often than not they stick to a single one, refurbishing it with reeds, grass, twigs and crowns of papyrus, as needs be. It's not particularly capacious, certainly not what you'd call a palace, unless you're a pigeon, but the view is always second to none. Barring coups and accidents they occupy this eyrie for the duration of their reign, which can span up to 24 years, just short of a silver jubilee.

The female usually lays two eggs, and the chicks hatch within a couple of days of each other. As befits their rank in the food chain, fish eagles are beneficent providers, and both chicks, sometimes three, are invariably fledged. The chicks do fight in the nest, especially in the early days, but the younger bird generally holds its own, and as they grow the squabbles peter out.

Both sexes utter the bird's famous call, throwing their heads back over their shoulders as though their message is meant for the gods in the skies above, as well as mere mortals. If the gods deign to reply, the eagles now keep the answer to themselves.

BLACK-BACKED JACKAL

The jackal-headed god Anubis played a pivotal role in the funerary rights of Ancient Egypt. He monitored the Scales of Truth to protect the dead from eternal death and conducted the Opening of the Mouth ceremony, among other important official duties. Anubis probably got the job by association, because jackals were always hanging around Egyptian burial grounds. This suggests that visibility and persistence can get you deified or at least elected to high office, even if you have a thin CV and dubious motives.

To be fair, jackals didn't actually apply for a job in the Egyptian pantheon, but they have always been granted the capacity for cunning. In African folk tales they are usually portrayed as tricksters who exploit the gullibility of other supposedly lovable and affable creatures. Such stories invariably end with the dimwit hero outwitting the jackal, an outcome that tends to disappoint cynics and leave lingering doubts about the efficacy of natural justice.

Having a name synonymous with treachery and deceit in popular culture is bad enough, but jackals have slid even further down the slippery slope of opprobrium. They are still regarded by some as vermin and hunted or poisoned in many areas of southern Africa, in effect becoming victims of their own success. Jackals live on their wits, something that has enabled them to survive, and even flourish, in areas outside game reserves, where other large carnivores were long ago exterminated to make way for sheep and people. The latter includes those folks who've still got plenty of bullets left over from killing the last lion.

Black-backed jackals are omnivorous, and, like most of us, they certainly enjoy lamb chops. Given the opportunity, they will prey on accessible livestock, especially those that are weak or incapacitated. However, by far the bulk of their diet consists of wild fare. Typical menus include lizards, insects, rodents, small mammals and even items as large as impala and juvenile wildebeest, the latter brought down in rarely witnessed cooperative hunts. They also chew grass to aid digestion and eat fruit and berries to the extent that the jackal-berry, a fruit-bearing tree, is named after them.

In game reserves where major carnivores are thankfully still alive and able to attend to their daily business, black-backed jackals are probably best known as highly nimble and opportunistic camp followers. They frequently shadow lions, hyenas and even the diminutive honey badger in anticipation of a free meal. They don't always wait at a kill until the formal diners have retired for brandy and cigars, being prepared to take the occasional big risk by darting in to snatch a morsel from within inches of a lion's massive paws, a liberty they don't usually take with leopards or cheetahs.

Despite their widespread distribution and familiarity, not a great deal is known about the black-backed jackal's social life beyond their immediate family. They've kept that largely under wraps, possibly because they're worried about the defamatory distortions we might come up with. They do drop the occasional enigmatic clue that things are not always as simple as they may appear. While they're usually seen alone or as a couple, jackals nevertheless exhibit some hierarchical and social behaviours normally associated with pack animals, including elaborate rituals of dominance and submission. Large groups can assemble out of nowhere to mob a predator or to take advantage of unusual bounty, responding to a vocal code we've yet to crack. There is even some anecdotal evidence that they share information about places to avoid.

Their family life is better understood. A female black-backed jackal selects a mate from several suitors, and the pair then settles into to a monogamous relationship that will normally last the rest of their lives. They both work hard to establish and maintain a territory – which varies in extent depending on seasonal and local conditions – by regularly using urine and faeces to define the border. Chasing out other home-hunting couples who don't read the signs or pretend they don't smell them is an irritating and ongoing chore. News soon gets around if one of the pair dies, and, with scant displays of sympathy, the survivor is chased off the property to make way for a new couple. Callous as this may seem, at the best of times desirable homes are in short supply, a problem familiar to young newlyweds the world over.

Three or four cubs, sometimes fewer or more, are born in early spring in an underground den, more often than not provided by an aardvark. The family may use two or three dens on their property when raising a family. The mother decides when it's time to move, and pops just has to go along with it, whether he sees the point or not. Even when they're only a few weeks old, the pups aren't carried by the scruff of the neck; instead mom entices them along with false promises of milk. It gets the job done and at the same time imparts a devious lesson taken straight from the jackal's practical book of life.

Young jackals share their parents' territory, gradually roaming further afield until they find a mate and then get to join the housing queue. While they're still around they help with rearing the next litter, contributing food and acting as babysitters. For reasons best known to jackals themselves, pups are born in the leanest season, and the extra help can make a big difference, with some studies suggesting that the number of helpers is directly related to the number of pups that make it to maturity.

Jackals are among the earliest and oldest members of the *Canis* genus, and they've had a long time to size us up. Excavations at a Stone Age human site in South Africa's Western Cape turned up fossil bones that were assumed to be those of dogs but on analysis proved to belong to a black-backed jackal. This find gives

a tantalizing hint that a semi-domestic arrangement of sorts may once have existed between our early forebears and the jackal. If it did, it didn't last. There is no evidence that dogs and jackals have ever interbred or that the black-backed jackal has ever been truly domesticated. Perhaps, like Anubis, they weighed us on the Scales of Truth and decided that we're not, after all, to be trusted.

OSTRICH

At some point in its evolutionary history, probably after the dinosaurs had punched out, the ostrich must have decided that the latest set of predators was a bunch of wimps. Rather than continuing to expend energy taking to the air in every minor emergency, it made up its mind to stick to the ground, grow enormous and have a crack at the bipedal land-speed record.

For a long time this kind of crazy explanation just didn't make sense to us. As a species, we've been dreaming about getting airborne since the days of Icarus and probably long before that. Even the odd australopithecine probably thought he'd finally worked it out, flapped his hairy arms and ended up as a squidgy mess at the bottom of a cliff. So who in their right mind would give up the ability to fly, if they had it? In consequence, it was long believed that ostriches had always been earthbound plodders. They had the right idea, even had the feathers, but otherwise never quite got their act together.

Recent DNA research seems finally to have proved that the ostrich's ancestors did hand back their pilots' licences after all. So did the forebears of the emu, cassowary and all the other flightless birds. It was a daring thing to do. Nature can get mighty ticked off if you return one of her gifts and it didn't work out for everyone. The elephant bird of Madagascar and the giant moa of New Zealand, both bigger than the ostrich, will not, alas, be joining us for lunch. But the ostrich, though never an avian Einstein, seems to have had a better plan.

The land-speed record for bipeds turned out to be a bit of breeze, 70 kilometres per hour with the top down. In theory, an ostrich can kiss goodbye to nearly all terrestrial predators except the cheetah. It can see them a mile away, no problem, because it is anything up to 2.7 metres tall and has eyes as big as its brain. Granted, operating such state-of-the-art optics takes up a sizeable chunk of its cerebral capacity, more than half by some estimates, so while the remaining synapses struggle to keep up, the ostrich is sometimes inclined to get a bit flustered and run around in circles. But if it inadvertently ends up running towards a predator instead of away from it, that's still not the end of the world. It has also evolved a kick that any fly half would sell his mother to possess, and feet with formidable single claws capable of disembowelling just about anything that tries to eat it.

Many folks in the Arab world think they're the dumbest bird they've ever come across and – let's not beat about the bush – nobody else has ever had particularly high expectations. Anything that swallows the kind of stuff an ostrich does must surely be a dumbass. The point in swallowing pebbles is to help with digestion, the kind of thing crocodiles do without ill effects. But ostriches tend to get carried away or distracted, at least in captivity, and gobble up all sorts of farmyard detritus. Having an elastic throat is all very well, but it doesn't mean that spark plugs, tin cans, bits of old rope and all kinds of other rubbish can be usefully passed down as grist to the mill. More than one ostrich autopsy has had veterinarians shaking their heads in disbelief. But we all have our quirks. Some of us, even the brainiest, routinely swallow copious amounts of slickly packaged ethanol, much to the astonishment and consternation of our livers.

Pliny the Elder was responsible for the most enduring and popular libel, claiming that ostriches hid their heads in the sand at the first sign of trouble. The point, he explained, was that the bird was stupid enough to believe that if it couldn't see anything, nothing could see it. Aristotle disagreed, but then again he had more or less made up his mind that the ostrich was some sort of avian-mammal hybrid, because it had eyelashes and a hairy neck. He wasn't entirely wrong. Unlike other birds, ostriches have indeed evolved some other mammal-like features: they urinate and defecate separately, as opposed to letting fly the splat that hits your car when you've just finished washing it. They've also been busy with modifications to their reproductive apparatus. If you want to hear more about that, write in and I'll send you the details in a plain wrapper.

Ostriches are prolific breeders; a female is capable of laying up to 100 gigantic eggs each year. Where circumstances dictate they're monogamous, but if his luck's in, a male can lord it over a harem of several females. Either way it's his job to build the nest. Clambering into a tree is out of the question, so the nest ends up being a nondescript scrape in the ground. The dominant female lays the first egg, and the others, if there are any, follow. They can

eventually assemble a clutch of up to 20 eggs. The leading lady sneaks back every now and again to make sure her eggs stay in the middle, presumably on the assumption that any predator will go for the outer ones first.

It was a common belief in the Middle Ages that ostriches incubate their eggs by staring at them, the heat of their gaze being quite sufficient. In reality they employ the conventional method. The hen, with her drab brown feathers, takes the day shift, and the male takes over in his black outfit during the night. It takes a biblical 40 days and 40 nights for the eggs to hatch. Pneumatic drills or pickaxes are not provided, so the chicks take two days to finally peck their way out of their colossal shells, not surprisingly emerging puffed and soaking wet.

We are all bound by the consequences of our ancestors' decisions and when born have little choice but to accept the world as we find it. Perhaps it's just as well that ostriches don't have the kind of brain that feeds the soul with doubt and introspection. If they did, chicks hiding from a raptor circling in the sky above would surely look to their own feathers and wonder why they'll never leave the earth and fly.

FUR SEAL

According to Celtic legend, Selkies are beings who live in the seas around Orkney and other remote isles to the north of Britain. They are indistinguishable from seals, but once ashore they shed their seal skins and take on human form. They are invariably gentle, wise and beautiful. If an islander meets a female Selkie on the beach and succeeds in stealing and hiding her seal-skin coat, she is obliged to remain with him as a loyal wife and bear him children, though she will always pine for the sea.

The legend betrays something of the loneliness of island life and also touches upon the curiously precarious status of seals. Unlike whales and dolphins, which evolved to give birth to their young at sea, seals were still hedging their bets in the Miocene. *Puijila darwini*, a fossil creature recently unearthed in Canada, has been hailed by science as the missing link in the evolution of seals, but it still had legs; it was equally adept at getting about on land as in the water, rather like an otter. The decision to opt for flippers must have come later, but even then the tricky issues relating to procreation were deferred for future generations.

Modern seals are now stuck between the sea and a hard place during the breeding season and could be forgiven for wondering whether their distant forebears had adequately thought things through. Flippers may allow seals to do as they please in the sea, but they're a bit of a flop when it comes to getting about on land. And pups are especially vulnerable on shore, even in the most desolate places, easily falling victim to land-based predators, like jackals and hyenas. Nevertheless, with a robust birth rate, these drawbacks were not a decisive issue until commercial hunters came along.

The first mariners to arrive at the Cape of Good Hope were mighty impressed by the 'unspeakable numbers' of seals they encountered, and over the years they did their best to address the situation. Their success can be measured by the fact that no populations of fur seals of practical use remained at the Cape when Jan van Riebeeck merrily stepped ashore in 1652. Undeterred, and ever with an eye on profit, Van Riebeeck promptly despatched the yacht *Goede Hoop* to Saldanha Bay to look for more. It soon returned with 2,700 pelts abandoned by French sealers who had clubbed so many that they couldn't find room for the discarded stock aboard their own ship.

Europeans had certainly had sufficient practice in seal clubbing by the time they reached the Fairest Cape. Starting in the years of the Roman Empire, Mediterranean monk seals were nudged ever closer to extinction by regular massacres, a relatively minor rehearsal for what was to follow around the world. Clubbing reached a frenetic pitch in the late 17th and the first half of the 18th centuries, when seals of all species were killed en masse for their pelts, meat and oil. The record was set by the captain and crew of the *Seringapatam*, which returned to London from the South Pacific island of Más a Tierra in 1801, its timbers groaning under the weight of 1 million pelts. The island, now renamed Isla Róbinson Crusoe, had been the castaway home of Andrew Selkirk, the real-life inspiration for Daniel Defoe's practical and innovative hero. This incidental fact demonstrates that even extreme isolation provided seals with little protection.

With an eye on tourism and their ears pinned back by the conservation lobby, governments now ban or tightly control seal hunting. Populations have recovered in some areas to the extent that seals are once again facing the age-old accusation of theft from the fishing industry, a global enterprise now beleaguered by the consequences of its own efficiency.

Like their counterparts around the world, Cape fur seals certainly eat plenty of fish; that's why their kind headed for the sea in the first place. In particular, they need to bulk up in time for the breeding season, the heftier the better. Big bulls get the prime seafront properties, and that's where the ladies like to be. If a bull arrives late or doesn't fancy squaring up to a 200-kilogram mountain of belligerent lard, he ends up in a modest estate on the rocks or at the back of the beach. With no view and restricted access to the sea, his bleak patch doesn't merit a second glance when the highly pregnant ladies waddle ashore. If that happens, the best plan is to forget about sex and go fishing, which is exactly what most young bachelors do.

Being around as a spectator for the unedifying squabbles between pregnant females probably isn't such a great idea anyway. Fights over the best spot within a male's desirable territory can be vicious, so much so that the resident bull sometimes has to heave himself up off the sofa and come over to help sort things out. Everyone eventually settles down, but the bull still has his work cut out, moving his substantial paunch between upwards of a couple of dozen moody females on his property to check they have everything they need. In between, he bellows at any neighbour who has the temerity to put a flipper over the property line. The mayhem goes on for six weeks, and he never has time for a sardine sandwich, let alone a proper lunch.

Females give birth within a few days of coming ashore, following a pregnancy of eight months. To get the dates right for the annual breeding cycle they employ a process known as delayed implantation, whereby the fertilized egg only begins to grow in the womb four months after impregnation. Within five or six days of giving birth they're ready to mate again, to the final and vociferous relief of the waiting bulls.

Bulls return to the sea when their task is done, but the mothers stay at the colony, leaving for two or three days at a time to forage. Seal milk has the highest fat content of that of any mammal, and so the pups rapidly put on weight and are usually weaned within 4–6 months. During this time they moult and put on the magic coat that so nearly became the undoing of their species.

'Not one is dissatisfied, not one is demented
with the mania of owning things,
Not one kneels to another, nor to his kind
that lived thousands of years ago,
Not one is respectable or unhappy over
the whole earth.'

From
I think I could turn and live with animals
by Walt Whitman